CONTENTS

preface

The growth of the Internet is phenomenal and its propensity to create money-making home-based business operations is equally staggering.

How does one go about launching such a business? Where do you start? How do you research the market? Where do you find the opportunities? What about start-up costs? Is it better to stick with one opportunity or hedge your bets with several? What are the available options for promotion? How do you create an Internet marketing strategy? Do you need to be an experienced Webmaster to succeed or can anyone participate? Which levels of Internet expertise are required?

This book provides the answers. But it also does more, much more, in a comprehensive review of 50 opportunities encompassing all levels of Internet expertise: skilled, semi-skilled and unskilled. Chapter 3 looks at 15 of the leading cyberspace reseller opportunities and in Chapter 4 you will be introduced to 35 ideas for a home-based Internet business, ideas that are already being successfully worked by other Networkers. In addition I always welcome direct approaches from individuals at my Web site **http://www.jimswebstore.freeservers.com** or via e-mail at **jimgreen@prweb.com**.

Can you *really* make money from a home-based Internet business?

Yes, you can, but how much will be governed by how well you apply yourself to preparation and how seriously you take your enterprise once you are up and running. Starting an Internet business at home is a whole new way of life that can be as exciting as it is rewarding.

one

Starting **out**

Starting an Internet business at home calls for precisely the same disciplines that you would face were you undertaking any other form of commercial venture:

- You must understand the nature of the marketplace.
- You must have a practical idea for your business.
- You must learn how to transform your idea into a reality.
- You must have a plan of action.
- You must have an appreciation of the tools you'll need.
- You must know where to locate them.
- You must learn how to use them.
- You must have a marketing strategy.
- You must learn how to sell on the Internet.
- You must manage your information efficiently to maintain progress.

At first glance this may look like a formidable list of things to do, but in fact there is nothing difficult about any of it. You may already be familiar with certain of these elements and the remainder you can learn for free as you progress in your initial planning. After that, it's all down to application, and application is the keynote to launching and successfully managing an Internet business at home.

What are the rewards once you get under way?

The answer to that question lies in how well you apply yourself to controlling a string of variables: how much pre-planning you will undertake; how seriously you will take your enterprise; how many hours you are prepared to put in to ensure success;

how proficient you will be in your marketing. Full time or part time, it makes no difference; the principles are the same.

Be assured though, you *can* make money if you give it your best shot because you will be competing on an equal footing in the global virtual marketplace. Competition for sales on the Internet is fierce, but then if there were no competition, there would be fewer opportunities to sell.

What is the motivation behind this astonishing phenomenon?

It is the facility the Internet offers to make money without having to engage in personal interaction and without the odious necessity of cajoling relatives, friends and neighbours into enlisting to form the core of an initial customer base.

However, as with any other commercial undertaking, you need a plan to ensure steady progress. Without some initial desk and field research and without taking the trouble to acquire an appreciation of the nature of the cyberspace marketplace, you will soon flounder.

Most of the millions of people worldwide currently plying their part-time trade as Netpreneurs are doing it for pin money, but there are others who've managed to transform what started out as a pastime into a lucrative full-time business. Some of these 'others' are earning high incomes and this is where you want to position yourself in time.

Even the pin money merchants have a plan, but the real home-based Netpreneurs have a master plan. You too will require a master plan if you are to succeed, and this book will provide you with all of the necessary ingredients to incorporate into a winning, masterly strategy for success in your home-based Internet business.

You are entering the fastest-growing industry in the world

The Internet is the fastest-growing industry in the history of the world and yet it is still in its infancy. It offers even the novice an opportunity to build a home-based business and compete with major commercial concerns around the globe. Given training, planning and consistent application, *anyone* with a computer can be successful.

With these elements in position, you can begin to create a business that will assist you in attaining your financial goals – and your independence.

Start thinking in terms of a realistic income

There are countless disparate ways to make money on the Internet but the reality is that it takes time and considerable effort to develop the available opportunities and to build a business that will sustain its momentum. You should start thinking in terms of what £50, £100 or £200 extra in your pocket could do for you and your family.

For some people it might represent the cash to pay for an overdue holiday or to meet mortgage repayments on time and without anxiety; for others this surplus might prove a godsend in covering running costs for the family car or paying for Christmas and birthday presents. Monthly incomes ranging from £50 to £200 are feasible in a short period of time for those who set about the task in hand with sincerity, proficiency and persistence.

It won't happen overnight, but if you apply yourself for two to three years you will create an opportunity to join the ranks of those successful home-based Internet business operators who are already enjoying sizeable annual incomes.

Which route will you take to create your business?

Working from home, there are basically four options at your disposal:

1. purveying your services as an expert or consultant in a designated field of commercial activity;
2. representing global concerns as an affiliate reseller of their produce (Chapter 3 presents 15 opportunities in this category);
3. concentrating your efforts on a home-based business idea already worked by other Internet users (Chapter 4 reviews 35 such opportunities);

4. combining (2) and (3) in an endeavour to create sustained prosperity, which is what your author does in his Networking activities.

This book focuses mainly on options (2), (3) and (4) because these are the areas:

■ where most home-based Networkers tend to operate;
■ where the opportunities would appear to exist for making the most money;
■ where you'll discover an abundance of free training and free tools to help you on your way.

Going it alone on the Web takes you into good company

Operating a home-based Internet business is a solitary occupation but you will be in good company because there are millions of you out there in cyberspace. Very soon it won't seem so lonely. You'll strike up friendships with all sorts of people you are unlikely ever to meet in person and you will experience generosity on an unbounded scale. You will be the receiver of freely given advice and practical assistance such as ideas for a suitable business, affiliate programmes, Web sites, virtual office suites, bulk mailers, domain name services, e-zines, mailing lists, e-mail facilities, autoresponders and ad submission tools – all of which you will not be asked to pay for.

This is the wonder of operating as an international Networker. Show willing, and you'll get lots of help and encouragement in your quest for success.

Can you think of any other business where you'd get these just for the asking:

■ free affiliate programmes (to resell top of the range produce globally);
■ free electronic ordering systems (to save you qualifying for merchant status);
■ free Web site construction tools (to help you build and promote your business);
■ free virtual office suites (to set you up as a cyberspace specialist);

- free bulk mailers (to post your promotional e-mails to prospects);
- free domain names (to personalize your e-mail/Web site addresses);
- free e-zines (to enhance your knowledge through electronic training);
- free mailing lists (to send announcements to targeted groups);
- free e-mail facilities (to cascade your marketing activities worldwide);
- free autoresponders (to reply instantly and automatically to enquiries);
- free ad submission tools (to blast out your ads to millions at one click)?

Basic skills you'll need

You do not need to be an experienced Webmaster to be successful in your home-based Internet operation. Quite the opposite, in point of fact – because too much knowledge might only serve to get in the way of free-flowing creative expression. However, there are several basic skills you will need to master. You may already possess sufficient expertise in most of them. The others you can pick up as you go along.

These basic skills are:

1. acceptable levels of literacy, numeracy and articulation;
2. computer literacy;
3. rudimentary comprehension of what the Internet is all about;
4. basic typing skills;
5. proficiency in receiving and sending e-mails;
6. ability to compose compelling sales copy;
7. working knowledge of the autoresponder facility;
8. competence in using electronic advertisement tools.

You should be au fait with points 1–5. As for the remainder…

Composing sales copy

This book is not the right place for an in-depth guide to composing good copy, but the Internet helps provide the answers. Here are two superb e-books (electronic books), which you should be able to download for free by sending an e-mail to each of the authors indicated below, requesting details of the appropriate Web sites for downloading:

How to Make your Ads Pull like Crazy! by Mark Hendricks
mark@hunteridge.com
Contains all you'll ever need to know on writing compelling sales copy for inclusion in your promotional e-mails and classified ads. It tells you how to find the people who will buy, how to write e-ad headlines, how to communicate your message, and magic words that transform your copy. This download also contains five of the most enlightened reports I've ever read on getting the best out of your Internet marketing efforts… and it's all for free!

Magic Letters: How to write so people buy! by Allen Says
allen@privatesites.com
Another remarkable piece of creative writing for which you can obtain reseller rights by payment of a small one-time fee. It provides practical guidance on issues such as: certain words that are irresistible; how to appeal to the subconscious; the rule of white space; how to educate, inform and sell more; increasing perceived value; simple words and short sentences that make money; how to create ideas in the reader's mind; the power of speaking with authority; how to be dramatic, bold and exciting.

Autoresponders and ad submission tools

Essential tools they may be, but mastery over them can wait until you become acquainted with the wizardry of these incredibly fast-working electronic devices. We'll be talking later about where to go to download as many of these as you wish.

You'll need a master plan in your quest for success

While you won't be submitting your plan to investment sources for start-up funding purposes (and you'll find out why in the

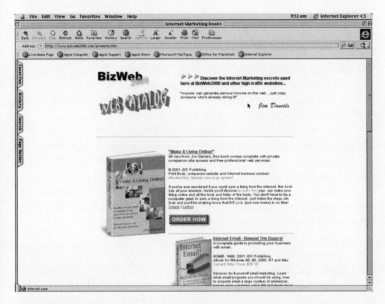

Figure 1.1 BizWeb catalogue of money-making ideas
(**http://www.bizweb2000.com**)

next section), it must nevertheless be sufficiently comprehensive
to enable you to set out your objectives clearly and concisely.
That way you will be completely focused on the reasons for
launching your enterprise. If you don't know where you are
going when you start out on your journey, you're hardly likely
ever to reach your destination.

Your plan will be in the nature of a report to yourself, and you
should make a start on it straight away. Don't wait until you
have located your opportunities. Do it now. You can fill in the
blanks later. Your plan should be a winning plan, a master plan
and, to achieve perfection, should comply with the detailed
instruction provided in Chapter 5.

Meantime, here is a list of the essential bandings under which
you will fill in the blanks as you progress in your start-up activities:

■ *Executive summary.* One single paragraph will suffice here.
  Tell yourself exactly what it is you are endeavouring to
  achieve and how you will go about it.

■ *Expertise.* List your skills and your levels of expertise. Make
  a note of the areas where improvement is required to
  enhance your skills quotient.

- *Opportunities to run with*. Fill this in when you have pinpointed the particular areas of opportunity you wish to pursue, develop and prosper from in your operation.
- *Objectives*. List your objectives for the embryo enterprise: whether personal or business, short- or long-term.
- *Competition*. Leave this section until such time as you have: (a) identified your opportunities; (b) achieved an inkling of the nature and extent of the competition.
- *Marketing strategy*. Complete this as soon as you are in a position so to do.
- *Marketplace*. Ditto.
- *Promotional options*. Ditto.
- *Production costs*. Ditto (but they should be nil or very, very little).
- *Strengths and weaknesses*. Ditto.
- *Financial projections*. Ditto.
- *Appendix*. This is where you stick all the bits and pieces of information you will accumulate as you go along in the early stages.

- Make a start on your master plan right now.
- Write down in simple terms exactly what you are endeavouring to achieve.
- Create the template now.
- Fill in the blanks later as your studies progress.

How about zero start-up costs?

Let's keep this section short and sweet by starting right away with the good news. If you go about matters the way I did in building my own Internet business, your start-up costs should amount to nothing. How come? There are a variety of reasons why this should be so, and if you follow the directions given throughout this book you will have cost yourself next to nothing in setting up as a home-based Internet business operator.

Freebies! Freebies! Freebies!

Follow the directions and start digging. The freebies will come at you from everywhere and your biggest problem will be to identify and discard those that you don't really need.

Free affiliate programmes

In Chapter 3 you will be introduced to some of the best selling 'bizops' (Internet shorthand for business opportunities) and, for almost all of them, it won't cost you a penny to join as an affiliate reseller.

Freeware

We've already touched on this subject but in Chapter 6 you'll discover how to locate all the freeware you'll need to build your business.

Let's look at the software you'll need

Later in the book we'll be discussing in detail the entire spectrum of the active Networker's software requirements: the various brands on offer, where to go for them, how to use them. Let's have a sneak preview now though at your basic Networking software needs:

- *Web sites*. Software? Yes, they are software items (for the purposes for which you will be using them at any rate). Notice Web sites plural. Should you decide to operate as an affiliate reseller, you'll need a few of them to house the aggregated programmes into which you'll be enticing other Web users to enlist, and to spread your OTS (opportunities-to-see) on the far-reaching worldwide Internet.
- *Virtual office suites*. You'll want several of these state-of-the-art electronic set-ups containing a fascinating range of useful tools: search engines, e-mail facilities, Web page design and creation systems, autoresponders, URL (Web site address) submission facilities and much more besides. You will also have the opportunity to make money giving away these suites to other opportunity seekers!
- *E-mail programmes*. Why would you want these when you'll already have them in your virtual office suites? You *will*. As you progress in your studies you will come to appreciate why you need designated e-mail programmes at your disposal as well as those incorporated in other software.
- *Autoresponders*. Likewise. Autoresponders are extremely efficient and you'll want to sign up for several. What do

they do? They reply instantly to enquirers with your pre-determined messages, as many as you wish, and in rotation at your command. Are they difficult to use? No. These systems are ultra-simple in execution.

- *Multiple search engine tools.* You'll want to promote your various Web site addresses frequently and consistently. Rather than do it manually, search engine by search engine, these electronic wonders reach hundreds of them at a time automatically and in a fraction of the time.
- *E-mail/ad submission tools.* These will blast out your promotional e-mails and ads to thousands in minutes.
- *Group mailers.* When you're posting your messages to groups of people (as you will), group mailers are indispensable.
- *Signature facilities.* A 'signature' is a sign-off promotional message you ought to include in all of your e-mails, business and personal. You never know who might bite when least expected. This piece of software will do it for you.

In your forthcoming searches for opportunities to promote, you will come across many priced offers for all of the foregoing. Do *not* be tempted to purchase any of them. In Chapter 6 I'll show you how to get them all for nothing and in the process save a sizeable sum of money. Do not rush out and buy the software. Wait for now and get it for free later.

Do some desk research before you start

It will pay you to undertake some minimal desk research before you embark upon cyberspace sourcing – not to find the opportunities, but to enhance your appreciation of the sheer scale of the facilities available to you on the Internet. You can best achieve this by referring to the undernoted publications, most of which you ought to be able to borrow from the Internet section of any main or central public lending library (and use their duplication services while you're there to copy any material of particular relevance):

Algie, Bob (1998) *How to Activate your Web site*, Ziff Davis, New York

Gray, M, Hodson, N and Gordon, G (1993) *Teleworking Explained*, John Wiley & Sons, New York

Johnson, Mike (1997) *Teleworking in Brief*, Butterworth/ Heinemann, London

Jones, Graham (1999) *Doing Business on the Internet*, How To Books, Oxford

Kent, Peter (2001) *The Complete Idiot's Guide to the Internet*, 7th edn, Prentice Hall Europe, London (no offence intended by the inclusion of this title!)

Mayo, Don (1998) *Internet in an Hour*, DDC Publishing, New York

Patterson, Marni C (1997) *Doing Business on the World Wide Web*, Ziff Davis, New York

Walker, Mark E (1997) *How to Use the Internet*, 4th edn, Ziff Davis, New York

Searching for opportunities

When the time comes around that you start to search in earnest for opportunities, the Internet itself is the place to go first. Another excellent source is to be located in the content of your incoming e-mails (which will increase in number as you get

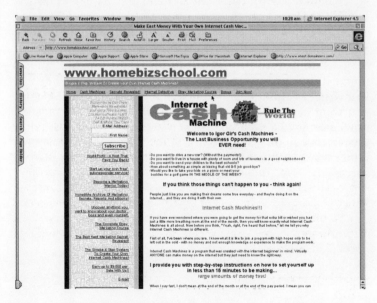

Figure 1.2 Home Business School: the place to earn while you learn (http://www.homebizschool.com)

going) and especially those e-mail messages emanating from other Networkers endeavouring to interest you in their own propositions. Do not delete any of these until you have digested the content. Many of them will contain gems of opportunity you might never otherwise encounter.

Steps and stairs to getting started

■ Decide on your basic *métier*: consultant, affiliate reseller or specialist business proposition.
■ Make an early start on your master plan for success.
■ Work on improving your skills quotient.
■ Investigate all free software options.
■ Master the art of writing copy for Internet promotion.
■ Undertake some basic desk and field research.

Exercise

Maybe you've considered launching a home-based business in the past. Maybe you've even gone ahead and started one but found it unfulfilling for whatever reason. Now consider this: you've got a computer and it could make some money for you if you went about matters in the right way. Take some time out now to come to a decision. If you went ahead, would you do it for pin money or would you do it to make some real money? Either way, start now on the beginnings of your master plan for success.

two

Where to **look for ideas**

Do you have a particular expertise? It doesn't matter what it is or how restrictive it may appear to you because you can bet there are thousands of other Internet users who would place a value on your expert knowledge. Is it a skill you would be prepared to share and make some money from?

Evaluate your own expertise

Ask yourself these questions:

- Do other people show an interest in your expertise?
- Would it have an appeal in cyberspace?
- Is it marketable?
- Could you sell it on the Internet?

If you answer yes on all four counts, you have just created a benchmark upon which to plan, launch and manage a home-based Internet business.

Look right in front of you

Here are three case studies to illustrate that looking right in front of you may well be all that is required to find a suitable idea:

- Seeing further than the end of his nose paid off handsomely for Douglas Maxwell. Douglas has been running the four-star Craigroyston Guest House in Pitlochry for over 17 years. Two years ago he signed on to the Net as a novice and, to enhance his limited knowledge of computer facilities, embarked on a series of training courses covering word processing, spreadsheets, databases and desktop publishing. Midway through his instruction he hit upon the idea of using the Internet to attract visitors to his guest house. It didn't take long to discover that cyber-communications were tailor-made for this business, and now 30 per cent of the Craigroyston reservations are made via Douglas's Web site.

▨ Angie's List was conceived and developed out a woman's frustration over no-shows and poor service from local tradespeople. So incensed was she that she set about researching, compiling and grading her own list of dependable operations, which just grew and grew. It now has a global significance as it contains thousands of recommended contractors in over 250 categories. You can learn more about Angie's List in Chapter 4, where it features as opportunity number 20 in a range of tried and tested ideas for a home-based Internet business.
http://www.angieslist.com

▨ Your author has a friend in Preston who is about to launch an interesting new home-based Internet business. He's retired now, but for over 40 years he worked as a sales representative and stayed at B & Bs all over the United Kingdom, not just once or twice but on repeat visits spanning all of his working life. Now he is putting his accumulated knowledge and experience to good use by constructing a Web site that will list in excess of 1,000 recommended B & Bs countrywide. His market focuses on overseas visitors, and (resulting from initial research) he has already formed valuable contacts in over 30 foreign tourist boards. The competition will be formidable but he has one distinct advantage over all of them – he's *actually* stayed in most of the establishments for which he will be providing details of location, amenities, rates, availability, etc.

Consult Web site directories

Another good source of information is the plethora of Web site directories now available in bookstores and public reference libraries. One of the best of these is *UK Directory*, the definitive guide to British sites on the Internet. It contains 70 pages listing over 2,000 business Web sites, and the range of interests and expertise covered is staggering. Spend some time researching this and similar directories because a good number of the entries relate to home-based operations.

If you have a skill, you could determine whether other people are doing it on the Internet and how they are doing it. If you're looking for an idea, you could establish what's on offer and whether there's anything that appeals to you.

Use the Internet search facilities

Using the search engines is another excellent option for sourcing ideas – but stick with the majors, otherwise you'll spend a lot of time going around in circles and getting nowhere fast. For best results, concentrate your initial searches on search engines such as Yahoo, Excite, Lycos, Infoseek, LookSmart, AltaVista, UK Plus and Dogpile.

Here is an example of what you might expect to find when you search using keywords and key phrases such as 'bizops', 'Internet bizops', 'Internet – business opportunities' and 'Internet – affiliate programmes'. The search engine employed for this example was Yahoo:

business and economy>small business information>keywords: Internet – affiliate programmes>26 sites

Just a few simple manoeuvres, a few seconds of your time, and you've hit the jackpot with 26 business opportunity sites (try out the formula above for yourself and you'll see what I mean). Best of all, the very first on the list fetches up Commission Junction – **http://www.commissionjunction.com** – offering a choice of 396 free affiliate reseller programmes with leading Internet retailers.

- Use the major search engines when you search for opportunities.
- Employ keywords and phrases.
- Follow the path of the Yahoo example illustrated above.
- Create your own path, eg 'business opportunities – Internet'.
- Print out those opportunities that interest you.

Scan the classifieds for golden opportunities

There are literally hundreds of thousands of classified ad Web sites on the Internet, some paid for, but most of them free of charge. They all represent valuable sources of information for the opportunity seeker in search of ideas. Here is a list of eight such sites:

- Micro
  http://linkplace.com/micro.cgi/1025–7585
- SmallBizFFA
  http://www.smallbizffa.net/ffa.pl?10100
- Ad Network
  http://www.adnetwork.nu/st/2635967.htm
- Leading Edge
  http://www.Websitings.com/classads/sites/2639315.htm
- FFANet
  http://www.ffanet.com/links/jim333.htm
- Autolink
  http://www.autolinkpro.com/index.cgi?47610

Make virtual visits to specialist opportunity shops

We visited a specialist opportunity house when Yahoo took us to Commission Junction. Now let your computer direct you on virtual visits to several of the dozens of other such operations to be found on the Internet. Here you will find opportunities in every conceivable product category.

While you're on the way, stop off at Jim Daniels's site.

http://www.bizweb2000.com

Jim quit his job in 1996 to become a home-based operator and is now acknowledged internationally as one of the leading Internet gurus. His book, *Insider Internet Marketing* (2000, Jim Daniels, Ohio), sells all over the world, and his helpful cyber-space marketing tips have assisted over 100,000 small and home-based businesses to profit online.

Specialist opportunity houses make a living out of promoting other people's programmes. Just one visit can net you hundreds of opportunities to consider.

Identify the openings

As you progress in your searches the data will begin to accumulate and this is when you should take time out to identify those opportunities with which you feel most comfortable. Don't make any hard-and-fast decisions yet. Just pencil in a few possibilities.

Review every option that comes your way

Leave this until the very last and at least until after you have read through the next two chapters. Discard nothing, because you will need most if not all of your located opportunities for an important exercise in test marketing.

Discovering gems in your electronic mailboxes

Once you are up and running you will soon create an Internet presence, and your incoming e-mail will gradually begin to increase in both quantity and quality. Check all your messages because you will discover some of importance. You will receive invitations to join affiliate reseller programmes, and also tips on free training, free software, free mailing lists, free virtual office suites, etc.

I was only a few weeks into my own Internet venture when I received an e-mail offering me free participation in a 10-week course of instruction on Internet marketing. The invitation came from an acknowledged leader in the field of Internet training and the knowledge I gained from this exercise proved extremely useful. It filled many gaps in my appreciation of the Internet and the instruction cost me absolutely nothing. Try it for yourself.

http://www.profitsvault.com

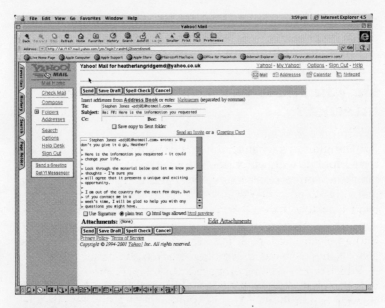

Figure 2.1 Look out for opportunities in your electronic mailboxes

Here is the syllabus for the free training course:

- introduction to Internet marketing;
- generating traffic with free reports;
- setting up your own free classified ad sites;
- effecting sales via your 'signature';
- composing persuasive e-mail messages;
- configuring e-mail programmes;
- where to find safe free opt-in lists;
- how to send out bulk mail without fear of spamming;
- marketing free affiliate programmes;
- the pros and cons of downline clubs;
- offline marketing.

There are many other free Internet training courses available. Look for invitations in your incoming e-mail:

- Never delete your e-mails before reading them through.
- Your e-mails will increase in quantity and quality as you progress.
- Feasible ideas for your embryo enterprise will just drop into your mailbox.

▓ Look out for offers of free training, free Web sites, free software, etc.

Do you know what sells best on the Internet?

Anything and everything that can be converted into an electronic format will sell on the Internet. Why? Simply this: the produce can be downloaded into the recipient's computer instantly. When someone makes the crucial decision to buy, they can't wait to get their hands on the merchandise. When that someone buys something on the Internet and it can be converted into an electronic format they can have it immediately, just as soon as they've handed over their credit card details.

Which types of selling proposition are of most interest to people who buy on the Internet? Whatever they perceive will make them smarter, happier, richer, healthier, more attractive, more popular: anything in fact that promises an enhanced lifestyle.

The single factor in common with all of these propositions (and with the majority of the opportunities you will encounter in your initial sourcing) is *information*, and information is the product category you would do well to focus on in your home-based Internet business:

▓ Information products are the top sellers on the Internet.
▓ Anything that can be converted into an electronic format is a front-runner.
▓ Lifestyle enhancement produce attracts Internet buyers.
▓ Instant receipt of purchase equals customer satisfaction.

Analysing the results of your initial searches

Do most of the opportunities centre on wealth creation? Do some of them have to do with reselling communications software, training programmes and electronic publications? It would be most surprising if you hadn't encountered all of these during your searches.

To illustrate the point, look at this recent survey published by the Harvard Business School, a survey that lists the top dozen affiliate reseller opportunity categories on the Internet:

1. wealth creation;
2. communications;
3. Internet training;
4. electronic publishing;
5. software programmes;
6. educational programmes;
7. online shopping malls;
8. personals/dating services;
9. credit card facilities;
10. banking;
11. gaming;
12. books (electronic and hard-copy formats).

Information is the core product marketed in almost every Web site category you can locate on the Internet, for example air, rail and sea travel, tourism, hotels, banking, insurance, postal and freight delivery tracking, credit card services, online malls and training. Moreover, those sites selling tangibles are totally reliant on the information they provide because prospects cannot see, touch or test the merchandise on offer: cars, furniture, furnishings, foodstuffs, clothes, etc.

Steps and stairs to finding an idea

▨ When searching for ideas for your business, start first with an evaluation of your own expertise.

▨ Look right in front of you. The best ideas are often so obvious that they may be discarded without due consideration.

▨ Consult Web site directories such as *UK Directory*.

▨ You can waste a lot of time on indiscriminate use of search engines. Stick with the majors and be precise in your keywords and key phrases.

▨ Review the classified ad Web sites listed in this chapter and sign up for a few while you're there. It costs nothing to join.

▨ It is possible to find just what you're looking for with a visit or two to the specialist opportunity houses.

▨ Identify the openings, review the options, but don't discard anything just yet.

▨ Your electronic mailboxes are gold mines of opportunity: programmes, software and training. And all for free.

▨ Information products are top sellers on the Internet.

Exercise

If you haven't already done so, complete the following:

▨ Undertake initial basic desk research at your local lending library.

▨ Spend some time on the major search engines, using effective keywords.

▨ Visit several classified ad Web sites.

▨ Look over everything that the Commission Junction Web site has to offer.

three

Introducing the
concept of affiliate reselling

We've touched on the matter several times already and now we will undertake an in-depth review of the entire concept of affiliate reselling to determine its feasibility as a candidate for a home-based Internet operation.

What is affiliate reselling?

In a nutshell: for 'affiliate reselling' read 'sales agency'. There are literally thousands of commercial concerns operating on the Internet that will grant you an agency and remunerate you on a commission basis to represent them and sell their produce through your own Internet marketing applications. In effect then, the term 'affiliate reseller' is simply universally accepted Internet jargon for sales agent.

Although the concept was first introduced on the Internet by a purveyor of tangible merchandise (Amazon Books), the produce is mainly information packages and participants make money in one of three ways:

■ selling the product online;
■ recruiting others to do likewise;
■ a combination of both.

These information packages (as evidenced in the Harvard Business School survey) centre on inducements to lifestyle enhancement.

The benefits of participation

Many established home-based business operators start out as affiliate resellers; some remain so, while others put the accumulated knowledge they glean from handling other people's business to developing an idea of their own.

There's a flexibility surrounding affiliate reselling that makes it an attractive proposition to newcomers to the Internet. Servicing several reliable and profitable programmes can evolve in time into a business in its own right while still enabling the reseller to progress to bigger things.

Why so many people set out on their Internet adventure as affiliate resellers can be summarized as follows:

- There is no long-term commitment.
- You can join many of these programmes free of charge.
- Where fees are applicable, they are usually modest and sometimes refundable.
- There are no trade restrictions.
- You may take on as many opportunities as you wish.
- There is no requirement to buy stock for resale.
- Marketing strategies and tools are provided free of charge.
- There is no personal interaction with prospects or customers.
- Commission statistics are normally available in real time online.
- Reimbursement is monthly by cheque or direct debit.
- There is no cash handling.
- There are no creditors.
- There are no debtors.

What to look out for before committing to a reseller opportunity

Visit the Web site and check out their credentials. Just one visit will suffice. If it's a professional operation it will display most if not all of the attributes listed above. For examples of how proven affiliate reseller programmes present their case, take a look at the Web sites for Cash Flow Club, Active Marketplace, Six Figure Income, Virtualis, Next Card and the other 10 opportunities listed a little further on in this chapter.

What to avoid

Disregard all downline clubs (save one) offering reseller status. You will spend a lot of time contributing to a giant list of prospects, which they will then sell to some other concern. The exception to the rule is the following truly excellent programme, because it teaches you how to efficiently market and build your very own downline of prospects for your own use, and at no cost. (A downline is a group of people actively participating in an Internet venture.)

The Duplicator

This programme is completely free to join and you are not required to buy or sell anything. You will receive a superbly designed and personalized multi-page Web site together with an informative wealth creation instruction manual. Your job is to promote The Duplicator and recruit other opportunity seekers to the programme, and in the process start to build your own first downline. You won't get paid but what you will get is a complete education programme on how to market and manage your Internet activities. Tom Wood invented this programme to build his own first downlines. He's now rich and famous, and pleased to share his incredible knowledge for free.

http://www.theduplicator.com/vip.cgi/jim333

How affiliate reselling works in practice

Operating a responsible affiliate programme is very simple. You are only replicating a formula already being successfully used by the company itself. Training is provided together with a host of electronic tools to enable you to be up and running almost immediately.

Professional concerns (such as the 15 recommended in this chapter) will set you up with all of the following:

- multi-page Web site (often personalized);
- hyperlinks and/or banners to your own site (if you have one);
- training manual;
- tips on how to get the best out of your marketing;
- essential tools;

■ secure ordering facility;
■ private members' area (company news, updates, developments, etc);
■ online commission tracking;
■ e-mail contact;
■ user name and password for confidentiality.

Ignore any opportunities you come across that do not provide these features because they are hardly worthy of consideration.

Why these features are so important

The multi-page Web site is identical in every respect to that of the programme contractor and, while it may be personalized with your ID, it contains all the facilities of the home site, ie full product range, secure ordering and merchant account facilities, e-mail contact, etc. All sales recorded are credited to you.

If you have your own Web site and opt instead to place a hypertext link or banner to promote the affiliate programme, you still have access to the full product range and ordering facilities. As soon as a prospect hits the link or banner, he or she is instantly transported to the programme's fully automated home site, where you are credited with the link and any ensuing action, ie a sale.

Before you start on promotion

Familiarize yourself with every aspect of the programme, the product or service, and the market at which it is aimed. If you spend some time on this before you start on promotional activities, the copy for your own particular slant on the sales message will flow more easily and you'll be able to answer any otherwise awkward questions thrown at you by prospects. You won't be interacting with prospects but they can reach you through the contact point at the Web site or in reply to your promotional e-mails. Be prepared before you leap in.

Devising your marketing strategy

Affiliate reseller programmes provide a basic marketing plan for the use of all participants, but to steal a march on the hundreds of others working the same proposition, you would do well to devise your own marketing strategy. Instruction on how to develop and implement this strategy is the subject of Chapter 8 but, to give you an early flavour, here is a rundown on the tools you'll be using to create an edge on fellow resellers:

- search engines;
- e-mail marketing;
- discussion groups;
- classified advertising;
- free reports;
- banners;
- signature messages;
- promotional CD ROM.

Always remember that you'll be open for business 24 hours a day, and your Web site cannot do it all on its own. It needs help from every relevant tool to nudge its message before prospects.

The value of links and banners

If you already have a Web site of your own and you join a reseller programme that offers either a hyperlink or a banner routed to the main promotional site, be sure to take up the invitation. Casual Internet surfers use these unique routed links on impulse, and every time one of them makes a purchase from your hyperlink or banner you get credit for the sale – and the commission. Routed hyperlinks can also be included in your e-mail marketing for other propositions.

Building up and using downlines to effect

As already stated, stay clear of so-called downline clubs but sign up free of charge for The Duplicator and make an early start on building up your own exclusive list of like-minded opportunity seekers. You may only attract a couple of dozen or so recruits in your early months of trading but if you promote consistently the numbers will increase in time to hundreds if not thousands.

This is how practitioners become 'heavy hitters', producing sales well above the average on every proposition they market. Add to that the additional split-level commissions earned on every piece of produce sold by your downline members.

Increase revenues of existing products and services

The reason why many home-based Internet operators remain in affiliate reselling after they've launched their own business is because advertising these opportunities for free is the easiest way to attract prospects to the primary business interest. When someone responds to an affiliate ad the opportunity is presented to strike up a dialogue and introduce the prospect to the main source of business.

Using the affiliate product or service yourself

Use the merchandise yourself where there is a repeat purchase factor in evidence. Order the product or service direct from your own Web site and the commission earned will represent a substantial saving on an already discounted price.

Why MLM isn't a dirty word on the Internet

In conventional networking the term MLM (multi-level marketing) has certain unfortunate connotations. Not so on the Internet. In fact MLM forms the backbone of all the affiliate reseller programmes you will encounter in searching for opportunities. If you decide not to participate in multi-level marketing in your home-based Internet operation, you may risk putting a curb on your earning power.

But what exactly is multi-level marketing?

Look upon MLM as cyclical selling, selling with many layers attached to it. It is not unlike the steps in an escalator: what goes down invariably comes back up. Put simply, the process is as follows:

1. Fred sells an MLM product or service to Tom.
2. Tom sells on the same service to Dick.
3. Dick sells it on to Harry.

So far, so good, but look what happens now. Every time Dick makes a sale, Tom gets a slice of the action. Every time Harry makes a sale, Dick gets a slice of the action and so too does Tom. Every time Harry's conversion sells on, Harry gets a cut and so too do Dick, Tom and Fred, and so on and on as they all continue to build their downlines. In a successful MLM operation, the selling and earning process is never-ending. It neither levels off nor does it flatten out.

With e-commerce one sale begs another, because what you will be doing in effect is replicating your own efforts many times over (through others) as you effortlessly build your downlines. That's the way it works on the Internet, and that's why all of the major programmes encourage and foster MLM among their affiliate members.

The benefits are threefold:

1. You build your downlines without ever having to interact with the participants.
2. You are credited with a percentage of their earnings on levels scaling 1–10 according to the nature of individual propositions.
3. You are relieved of the responsibility of collecting monies personally because the programme contractors handle that onerous task and remunerate you monthly by cheque or direct debit.

All the time, of course, you are also earning in your own right through your own personal promotional efforts.

MLM is good for your Internet business, allowing you to:

▓ continue to make money from your own promotional activities;
▓ build your downlines effortlessly;
▓ earn additional income on a range of affiliate levels.

Undertake an objective overview

If by now you feel you might like to try your hand at affiliate reselling, you ought first to undertake an objective view of the sheer range of opportunities available globally. You can accomplish this easily by spending some time at a unique Web site that lists over 3,000 affiliate reseller programmes.

http://www.AssociatePrograms.com

Look first at the categories, choose one of particular interest and then review a dozen or so relevant Web sites.

Reviewing 15 proven opportunities

It follows quite naturally then that the top affiliate programmes reflect the most popular reseller opportunity categories listed earlier. These programmes have all been around for some years, and they are tried and tested favourites among global opportunity seekers.

You may already have visited several of these Web sites in your searches. If not, you should make a point of looking over all of them as soon as possible. Where potential income is indicated, the amounts quoted are gauged from the author's own personal experience of programme participation. Bear in mind though that no two people will have the same experience. The amounts you earn are down to how much time and effort you are prepared to put in.

Wealth creation

1 – Cash Flow Club Online (CFCO)

Here is a series of remarkable opportunities (rolled into one) for anyone in the process of setting up a home-based Internet business. CFCO takes all that is best from affiliate reselling and Internet marketing, and combines the concepts of both into a series of 10 unique interlinking Web sites. The results are revolutionary and CFCO is currently taking cyberspace marketing into dramatic new global dimensions.

The primary vehicle (which you should look at first) is **http://www.cashflowclubonline.com/?JIM101299** where for a one-off *donation* of $50 (around £33) members receive a complete package comprising:

▨ comprehensive training on Internet marketing;
▨ instruction on wealth-building strategies;

- staged cash grants totalling $1,900 (£1,267);
- $300 (£200) subscription (paid for) into self-liquidating loans programme;
- free entry into $1,000 (£667) value StarMax fully automated Internet business, which CFCO claims will generate an average minimum weekly income of $400 (£267);
- involvement in third-world poverty relief initiatives;
- free entry into online investments programme.

These membership benefits occur in a staged process: ongoing training, cash grants and self-liquidating loans, followed by entry into various subsidiary programmes (fully automated Internet business, investment programme, etc).

The real money-spinner is the self-liquidating loans programme. This is only open to Cash Flow Club members, and you can enter immediately by paying a combined subscription fee of $350 (£233). Loans start one month after receipt of funds.

http://www.cashflowloanonline.com/?JIM101299

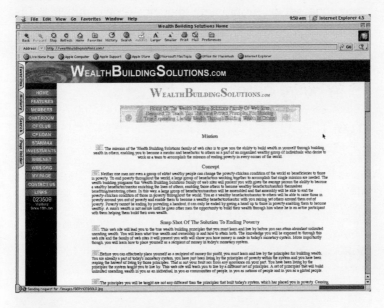

Figure 3.1 Gateway to a series of wealth-creating solutions (**http://www.wealthbuildingsolutions.com/?JIM101299**)

Read every word on every page of both Web sites; then read them all again – and again. On the third reading a light should switch on in your head. Should you decide to subscribe to either or both of these programmes, use the above URLs *exactly* as spelt out because you are only permitted to join through the auspices of an existing member. You'll find an overview of both these programmes on the Web site below.

http://www.wealthbuildingsolutions.com/?JIM101299

2 – Active Marketplace

Personally orchestrated by Declan Dunn, a multimillionaire Internet guru in his own right, 'Winning the Affiliate Game' is the system you will be selling in his free-to-join programme. There is 50 per cent commission on your own sales and 10 per cent on those of your downline.

http://www.activemarketplace.com/w.cgi?winning-6556

This is an extremely popular product with Internet opportunity seekers and one that consistently attracts favourable media coverage. You would do well to purchase it yourself before going on to sell the programme to others. It's a complete guide on how to be a successful reseller. Sample the product first and after a short settling-in period you could be earning between £150 and £200 per month.

3 – Six Figure Income

Brainchild of Gery Carson, yet another Internet high-flyer, the SFI wealth-creation study course is currently operating in 140 countries worldwide. There is no cost to enrol, and the programme features a 'quick-pay' compensation plan that pays out 65 per cent on the first three levels.

http://www.sixfigureincome.com/?122341

Potential earnings are around £100 per month.

Communications

4 – Virtualis

This features a breathtaking 22-page Web site reselling what many experts consider the finest range of virtual servers on the Internet. This is a prestigious communications programme and

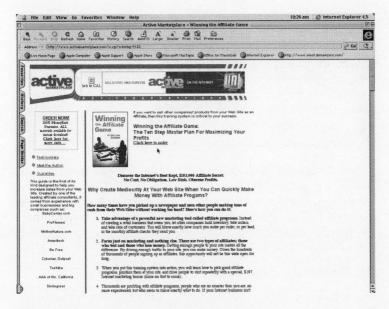

Figure 3.2 Complete guide to how to become a successful reseller (**http://www.activemarketplace.com**)

remunerates affiliates in two ways: commission on direct sales of produce and commission on recruitment of downline affiliates. It is free to join, but you'll need to demonstrate some basic product knowledge before they'll let you in on their secrets to making money, ie you are asked to sit an online exam.

http://www.virtualis.com/vr2/jgreen2

This one is a slow burner to begin with and, although many experienced Virtualis resellers command huge commission payouts, do not expect to earn more than £50 per month for some considerable time.

Internet training

5 – Site Sell

This programme would fit equally well under the 'wealth creation' category, and it's one of the best bizops on the Internet. Affiliates earn excellent commission reselling a 400-page e-book *MYSS My Site Sells*, which contains astonishing information on how to galvanize the average Web site into a top moneyspinner. A strongly recommended opportunity and free to join.

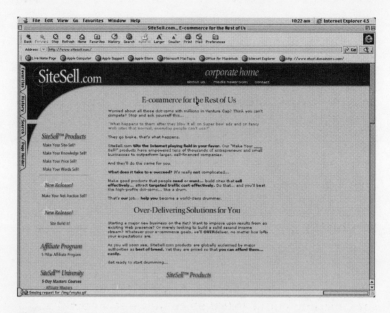

Figure 3.3 Comprehensive instruction course on how to make your Web site irresistible (**http://www.sitesell.com**)

http://www.sitesell.com/success66.html

This is another slow burner. However, if you stick rigidly to the marketing plan the sales will come, with a potential monthly income of £150 to £200.

6 – Marketing Tips

Corey Rudl started his Internet business from a tiny room some five years ago, made some mistakes as we all do in the beginning, learnt from them and is now turning over millions annually. He put his accumulated knowledge to good use when he devised Marketing Tips – a remarkable opportunity that offers Internet newcomers a series of free lessons, which he previously sold for $147 (approx £100). Take advantage of his generosity and, if you decide to sign up for his full-scale programme (which costs approximately £165), he will teach you how to make a great deal of money on the Web.

http://www.marketingtips.com

7 – Profits Vault

This one is an Aladdin's Cave of cyberspace information products: e-books, reports, courses of instruction – and how to sell them, in a series of easy-to-digest guides. There's a one-time subscription fee of around £30, which opens up the way to multiple income streams with detailed instructions on successful application. Even if you decide not to invest, you will still be offered several free courses of valuable instruction on how to implement the essential aspects of Internet marketing. Here's the Web site and it's well worth a visit.

http://www.profitsvault.com

Promotional

8 – Blast4cash

How to get loads of traffic with sensational promotion tools: 1,000,000 search engines and directories, and 18,000 classified ad sites, blasting out to 15,000 other sites – all to build you a gigantic mailing list, and you get paid for compiling it. Costs £7 to join.

http://blast4cash.net/member/singles

Software

9 – Postmaster

A product of Online Automation Inc, this postmaster will pay you to work for him! It's state-of-the-art Internet software, and free to join.

http://post-master.net/rs/jimswebstore

Educational

10 – BizOppAlliance

If you're new to affiliate marketing, this is the site for you. Earn as you learn from the professionals. Free to join.

http://www.bizoppalliance.com/?id=25324

Figure 3.4   This Postmaster will pay you handsomely to work for him (**http://post-master.net**)

11 – Magic Learning

This family product consists of a series of learning systems. It pays well, and there is no fee to join as an affiliate reseller.

http://www.magiclearning.com/cgi/members/JG51079

Personals

12 – One and Only Network

Start a virtual introduction agency without the trouble of client contact. It works well, and pays out very good commission. Free to join.

http://www.one-and-only.com

People get rich in the USA working this programme but it's early days yet in the United Kingdom for the One and Only Network. However, if the US experience is anything to go by, signing up for it now may pay off handsomely in the future as the programme builds momentum.

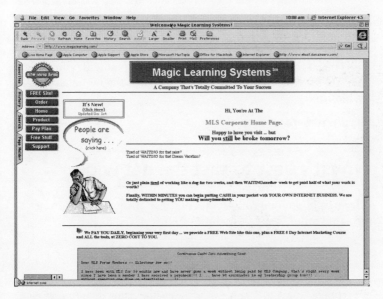

Figure 3.5 Family product consisting of a series of learning systems
(**http://www.magiclearning.com**)

Credit cards

13 – Next Card

This is a low-cost credit card facility that is sweeping the USA. It is not yet available in the United Kingdom, but you can obtain global reseller rights for free.

http://cognigen.net/getnext.cgi

You won't build a business on Next Card, but it makes a nice addition to your portfolio and has the potential to attract interest in your other propositions.

Banking

14 – Clickbank

This is the online banking system that offers a range of services: secure ordering, merchant status, credit cards, etc. It is worth joining. No fee required.

http://www.clickbank.com

Books

15 – Amazon

This famous online bookseller will provide you with a link to its Web site for free. It is worth considering for the name alone. No fee required.

http://www.amazon.co.uk

Why it's best to cast the net wide

Why would anyone run several of these affiliate programmes at the same time? Reasons include:

- The investment is modest.
- It costs nothing to service them.
- They're not cluttering up your computer.
- They're working 24 hours a day, every day, in cyberspace.

It will pay you in the early days to review as many opportunities as you can find, sign up for those that appeal to you and run with all of them for a time: perhaps as much as 12 months. When you start out, you will have no idea as to which types of programme work best, when they work or even why they work.

There's a seasonal aspect to some of them. Although wealth-creation programmes are popular all year round, they peak twice a year: at the beginning of January and at the close of the holiday season when opportunity seekers get a rush of blood to the head, probably brought about by the thought of impecunious times ahead. Online dating service programmes start buzzing at the outset of spring when young men turn their thoughts to you-know-what...

You have to cast your net far and wide, hedge your bets, take note of individual programme progress and allow time for the programme to run its course. Look at it this way. If you are monitoring six affiliate programmes in your portfolio and each of them turns over only £50 per month, your computer will then be effortlessly providing you with additional monthly income of £300.

Some of these programmes you will discard in time, others will develop into regular income generators and one of them might even make you wealthy.

- Evaluate every opportunity you come across.
- Sign up for as many as appeal to you.
- Test them all out on a trial basis.
- Take note of seasonal variations.
- Earn while you learn.

What happens if you decide to specialize straight away?

You run the risk of early disillusion with your project if you do, because the odds of spotting a winner straight off are minimal. Some opportunities seem better than others (it's all to do with presentation) and you'll come across one where you think: this is it; this is the one; drop everything else and go for it. Don't be tempted. Don't be unduly swayed by the packaging. Stick with them all for a time because it might be one of the boring ones that pays off best in the end.

How come they let you join for free?

Whenever I'm asked what it costs to set up as a home-based Internet operator and I reply 'Nothing', the response is invariably 'I don't believe you. There has to be a catch. No one gives anything away for nothing.' That's true; no commercial concern ever really gives anything away for free.

But there's no catch, only a very good reason for the magnanimity of the programme contractors: promotion. Concerted, consistent, continuous global promotion is so vital to the reseller programme contractors that they gladly and freely dispense pre-designed, personalized Web sites, e-mail facilities, auto-responders, search engines, submission tools and free entry to their programmes when they could easily charge at least a token fee for all of this.

Why? Because every time you send out a promotional e-mail, place free classified ads, submit Web site addresses to the search engines, blast out your automated messages to enquirers, you are not just marketing your own enterprise – but essentially you are marketing and promoting *their* corporate programmes.

Learning from the competition

We talked earlier about finding nuggets among the dross in your incoming e-mails. You can learn and accumulate an enormous amount of valuable information about money-making opportunities from the competition: not only from e-mails but also from the millions of classified ads that infest the Internet. Take time out to study some of these and take note of those opportunities you haven't come across in your own searches.

Look too at how other operators promote their propositions, the media they use and how they compose their sales messages. Some of the copy platforms are questionable, some downright naive, but some will inspire you and prompt you to look more closely at your own approach.

Promotion is what it's all about, and the ability to compose compelling sales copy is the key. We'll examine promotion in Chapter 8.

■ Look at what the competition are offering.
■ Observe their marketing methods.
■ Learn from the good and the bad in their ad copy approach.

Maintaining essential records

As the information begins to build on your findings, you'll want to devise a simple system to keep track of it all and to allow for ready access in various circumstances. If this measure is not instigated at an early stage, it can all run away from you very quickly. There's too much of it to carry around in your head, and if lost or misplaced, the retrieval of information will take time and cause you unnecessary aggravation.

Although your business will be managed through electronic data applications, I recommend a hard-copy register to house all of this essential stuff, because that will allow you to refer to your findings when you're not at your computer.

What sort of data will this register contain? It should include:

■ income-generating Web sites;
■ functional Web sites (ie virtual office suites);
■ classified ad Web sites;

- Web sites under construction (ie composite sites you are currently building);
- e-mail addresses;
- autoresponder facilities;
- commission scales (for individual opportunities);
- user names and passwords (ie for access to revenue statistics on individual programmes);
- advertisement submission tools;
- schedule of promotion (ie daily/weekly ad and e-mail postings).

You'll get more details and examples on how to construct these sections when we arrive at Chapter 9.

Steps and stairs to affiliate reselling

- People use the Internet as a source of free information but they'll also pay for it if the product promises enhancement of lifestyle.
- Look for products that fulfil this promise.
- Choose several opportunities from the main product categories and run with them all for a time on a pilot basis.
- It's a mistake to throw all your energies behind one opportunity until you are convinced of its effectiveness.
- Promotion is essential to success on the Internet and that is why the reseller contractors give so much away for free in return for a promise from you on promotional activity.
- Learn from the competition: capitalize on what they're doing right and avoid repeating their mistakes.

Exercise

From the selection of opportunities you have located so far, choose the one that currently appeals to you most. Go to the programme Web site, pull down and print out every page and every link to ancillary information that you can find. Study all of these in detail and make initial assessments on the product or service:

■ viability;
■ user-friendliness;
■ value for money;
■ exclusivity;
■ ease of purchase.

Now repeat the process for several others among your range of possibilities. This exercise will give you a 'feel' for handling a variety of opportunities in one portfolio.

four

Thirty-five **ideas for a home-based Internet business**

If you cannot come up with an idea of your own or you don't fancy affiliate reselling, here are 35 alternative opportunities worthy of your consideration. Whatever level of Internet expertise you currently possess, there's a business you could start at home in this extensive selection. Among the examples are opportunities for the highly skilled, the semi-skilled, the totally unskilled – and with appropriate planning you could run several of these businesses concurrently. They're as new as the Internet itself *but* they are all being successfully worked by home-based operators like yourself.

Many of the descriptions that follow contain URLs that will take you to Web sites where you can learn more – or see for yourself how someone else is marketing the opportunity. For those businesses that take your fancy but for which you are short on skills, there is ample training available online and usually for free. How much income you can expect to make is down to the quality of your planning, your willingness to learn and your application.

1 – The six-figure Internet publishing plan

A couple of years ago a woman came up with a very simple but powerful method for making money on the Internet – *a method that anyone can copy and profit from*. Here is what she did.

On America On Line (AOL) there is a forum called 'Business Know How'. Within this forum there is a section 'File Libraries'. The file libraries contain articles that people have uploaded (posted) to the forum. These people may be marketing consultants, software publishers, book publishers or writers, or other experts. They post the articles in order to get exposure to Internet users who may be interested in their services. By looking at the download statistics for the articles, the lady in question was able to determine which reports were the most popular with members of the forum.

As a matter of fact, the number of times a file is downloaded is posted right on the main screen, and since you can sort the articles by number of downloads it is an easy task to find the most popular titles. Now, these articles are usually only three or four pages long but they contain a wealth of information on just about everything to do with operating a business, including advertising, management, pricing, start-ups, business plans, organization, marketing, etc.

She downloaded several of the most promising articles and wrote to the authors to ask for two things: 1) permission to reprint the reports on floppy disk; 2) permission to transfer the reprint rights to others. Now, why on earth would these authors give her permission to reprint their copyrighted material? For the same reason they had uploaded the articles in the first place: free publicity. They know that the more people who view their articles, the more exposure they will get for their products and services – and the better chance they have of making a sale. For them, it's free advertising – and for her, it represents a never-ending source of fresh, new reports.

After she got permission from the authors to reprint their articles, she grouped them together according to subject matter and produced 12 disks that featured a different business topic. Each disk contained five to eight different reports relating to the topic. At the bottom of each report there is a 'plug' for the author. This plug is sometimes called a resource box and generally contains the author's name, contact reference and information about the product or service on offer. It looks just like a classified ad.

Now (bearing in mind that the lady is selling reports, not the product or service) this is where she was really clever. Instead of just selling the disks herself, she came up with the idea of an opportunity catalogue and offered the disks for sale in four different ways:

- *Retail.* You could buy each disk for $8.
- *Reprint.* You could buy the reprint rights to a disk for between $100 and $150 and sell the disk to others at retail.
- *Unlimited.* You could buy the reprint rights to a disk and also the right to sell the reprint rights to others. This option cost $180 to $250 depending on the disk.
- *Business in a Box.* If you were really serious about making money, you could buy the Business in a Box, which included unlimited reprint and resell rights to all the disks for $2,000. Many people went for the Business in a Box option because she included a discount coupon for $1,000 if they ordered within a certain date that was stamped in red on the coupon. The last I heard, she had sold 100 Business in a Box packages for $1,000 each in less than a year. Total turnover $100,000.

Anyone could do what this lady did because there are literally hundreds of thousands of valuable, informative free reports and dissertations on the Internet – and all of these are there just waiting to be downloaded and marketed successfully.

At first glance this might appear like a convoluted way to do business, but in reality it is very simple – and it's a proven winner. There are unlimited numbers of authoritative, well-written, free reports available for download on the Internet, reports from authors who are only too willing to let you have them to do with as you please.

2 – Start an Internet advertising agency

If you are motivated and highly competent in using and explaining the workings of the Internet to small businesses in your locality, you could build up a home-based Internet ad agency serving clients in a specialized area. The best way to start is to focus on a market with which you are familiar. You could, for example, set up a Web site to attract advertising from the travel and tourism industry, or you could specialize in one type of service. For example, a Web site devoted to wedding planning will attract advertising revenue from hotels, restaurants, florists, car hire, bakeries, etc.

How you make money

You can lease a virtual server that will hold 5,000 pages (or more) for around £140 per month. If you offer your clients designed, maintained Web pages at £20 per page, you will only need to sell seven pages to meet this expense. The goal must be to get as many clients as you can, thus maximizing the profitability of your server capacity.

You can also offer custom design services on an hourly basis. Charge between £100 and £150 per hour – or determine your rates on a per-job basis, taking into account all billable hours involved in the project. Many Internet ad agencies also work on monthly retainers of £500 or more, providing updating and maintenance. An example of this might be updating the menu on a restaurant Web page.

In essence, your incomings derive from: (a) advertising revenue; and (b) a mix of hosting/design/maintenance fees.

To get started, you'll need to set up some sample ads on your domain to show to potential clients. This is a business with enormous growth potential where you can develop a close relationship with your clientele. You'll be servicing an area you know about and enjoy – but remember that (as a one-person agency) you must be hands-on in every aspect of the process, from selling ads to designing and maintaining the Web pages.

Maybe you're now retired and maybe you worked in or managed a traditional advertising agency during your 'active' years. Here's an opportunity to do it all over again from home as a cyberspace specialist.

3 – Set up your own clip art business

Clip arts are those ready-to-use illustrations, borders, stylized headlines and other little pieces of art that you clip out to brighten up ads, leaflets, newsletters, etc. Before the emergence of new age electronic technology, the main sources for clip art were office supply stores and mail-order dealers. Now you can pull down a sizeable quantity from your computer, and an even bigger selection from the Internet. And all for free.

Moreover, there are many software packages now available for free download on the Internet that will permit you to create your own copyright-free graphics, which you can sell on to other users.

The clip art business isn't everyone's cup of tea but, if there's a creative streak in you bursting to break out, you might do very well in this home-based opportunity to make money on the Internet.

4 – Become a home-based desktop publisher

According to recent research findings, this market has expanded globally from £1.8 million in annual sales in 1985 to almost £3.1 billion in 2000 – and there would appear to be no end in sight to this phenomenal growth. One of the very real challenges of this business is that there are still millions of potential clients out there who are still unaware that they need the services of a desktop specialist. Home-based desktop publishers are engaged in producing a welter of graphic materials: brochures, flyers, advertisements, newsletters, books, business proposals and forms. Some also provide word-processing services for their clients, while others will work on almost any type of graphic assignment.

This is an enormous market where the proficient home-based operator can locate endless opportunities for residual income. It's a superb business for homeworkers who have the technical know-how, enthusiasm and will to succeed.

5 – Sell information packages you get for free

Here is a ready-made business you could be operating from home within a month. You can own and sell the reproduction rights to five popular information products – and all for free. The products come free of charge and all it will cost you to get going is the carriage charge of approximately £2 per product. Moreover, your promotional costs will be minimal because your marketing strategy would consist of:

- e-zine advertising;
- e-mail campaigning on a daily basis to free opt-in lists;
- newsgroups;
- personal Web site promotion.

If you sold 50 of these information packages in a month at £12.50 each (almost half the recommended selling price) you would net £625.

Study the detailed outline on the publisher's Web site and decide for yourself.

http://www.rjcampbell.com/

6 – Create, register and auction domain names for free

Some time ago the UK national daily press carried a story about an enterprising young man who exercised considerable foresight when he registered the domain name **http://www. bettingshop.com.** Why? Because a few months later he sold it in an Internet auction for £25,000! The trick is to locate and register domain names that are likely to appeal to certain big businesses or institutions, which will pay handsomely for the rights.

Until very recently the fees involved in registering a bundle of likely names proved prohibitive. Not any more. There's a new Web site where for a small fee you may register as many names for business and personal use as you wish.

Why not get your thinking cap on? Come up with some likely candidates, visit this Web site and start registering. Who knows, there might be £25,000 – and a business – in it for you.

http://ehost.domainzero.com

Alternatively, you could do a similar thing the following way – but it will cost you more. Every week thousands of people have their valuable, treasured dot.com names repossessed because of non-payment of the domain registration fee. If InterNIC (the worldwide registration authority) do not receive payment by the due date, they repossess the domain name in question and return it to the pool of available names. Unclaimed Domains compiles a weekly list of these expired names and provides access to it for a fee of around £30 per year. Affiliates make £18 commission on every sale.

http://unclaimeddomains.com

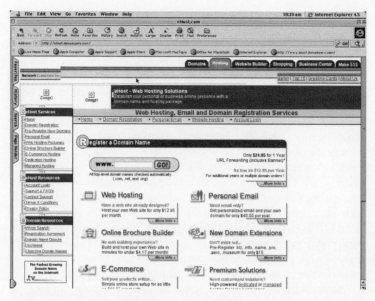

Figure 4.1 How to make money registering and auctioning domain names (**http://ehost.domainzero.com**)

7 – You can start in this business for under £10

This is a simple four-step system you can set up to create your own mini home-based Internet business. It will cost you just $14.97 (almost £10) and here is the exclusive set-up information you will receive:

- how to create your Internet cash machines with no money;
- how to get others to do all the work for you;
- how to accept credit cards immediately with no set-up charge;
- how to take easy advantage of what people look for in the search engines;
- how to make back-end profits every month;
- how to get a free e-book maker.

The system comes complete with your own personalized Web site, merchant status and free resell rights allowing you to sell the product for what you paid for it – and pocket all the receipts. This might seem like an affiliate reseller opportunity, but it's not, because you keep all the profits. To enter this business, send an e-mail to jjjones@infowave2000.com with 'Internet Cash Machines' in the subject line. Alternatively, you can view the entire range of Mr Jones's money-making opportunities by visiting the following Web site:

http://www.infowave2000.com

The following four ideas are for businesses you can operate as a home-based e-zine publisher. E-zines are electronic magazines in newsletter format (list of topics, articles, tips, etc), which are e-mailed to subscribers. They are generally offered free of charge, but recently a few niche e-zines have emerged that command fees for subscription because of their unusually high quality of content. E-zines are considered by many to be the real 'work horses' of the Internet because more and more promoters are discovering that Web sites are *not necessarily* the best way to generate sales in cyber-space. There are two reasons why e-zines might be considered as more efficient tools than Web sites at generating sales.

Firstly, with a Web site it is very easy for visitors to become distracted and leave your site before they've taken the time to read the sales pitch. After all, they have the world at their fingertips. With an e-zine, on the other hand, you have the opportunity to reach your prospects at times when they are not so liable to be distracted. This way the chances of your material being read are substantially enhanced. Since most users still access the Internet through a dial-up account, they can read your e-zine anytime, even when they're not online. Once received, your message stays in the mailbox until deleted.

Secondly, e-zines allow you to build relationships with your readers because they will be seeing your publication on a regular basis. This consistency leads to sales.

Let's now examine the profit streams your e-zine can tap into.

8 – Sell advertising in your e-zine

This is far and away the most popular method of generating income with an e-zine. Indeed, you would be hard pressed to come across an e-zine that does not sell advertising in one form or another:

- *Classified ads*. These are short, pithy ads generally grouped together at the end or interspersed throughout the articles.

■ *Sponsorship*. Sponsorship ads appear at the very beginning, and sponsors invariably have exclusivity, which allows the e-zine owner to set higher rates for the inclusion of such ads.

■ *Direct mail*. This is where an e-zine publisher e-mails an ad to the entire subscriber list or part of it. While this can be lucrative for publishers, they must always guard against saturating their subscriber lists with offers. Direct mail works best when lists are large. With 30,000 subscribers on tap, publishers can sell six direct mailings of 5,000 each per week. That way they can be certain that no one on the list receives more than one promotional e-mail per week.

Successful home-based e-zine publishers make an annual residual income into five figures from the ad revenue they pull in.

9 – Promote your own products and services

More and more Internet users are coming to realize the advantage of promoting their goods and services via *their own e-zine* – and with good reason. Professionally produced e-zines are popular visitors to electronic mailboxes worldwide.

An effective promotional method is to publish an article in every issue focusing on a single benefit the reader will enjoy by owning or using your service. But don't write *sales* letters. These articles should be rich in content and give your readers valuable information while at the same time highlighting the reasons why they should buy. Give them some 'insider secrets'; show them how they would use your product or service to save time or money.

Imagine you have an e-zine with 30,000 subscribers and you sell a product to just one-tenth of 1 per cent of them in each weekly issue. A product retailing at £5 would produce £150 income every month.

Don't preach; don't write sales letters; let your well-couched, informative articles act as hidden persuaders in attracting incremental sales.

10 – Provide a product endorsement service

Do you miss out because you don't have a product or service of your own? Not necessarily. There are numerous traders who would love to give you a piece of the action if you agree to promote their merchandise to readers of your e-zine. In general terms, you split the proceeds 50/50 with the product owner.

Product endorsement works best when:

- You work with traders who have products that closely match the interests of your readership. If you publish an e-zine relating to the grooming of dogs, a good product would be a book, CD ROM or video on dog training – and, better still, something entitled 'Dog Grooming Secrets of the Professionals'. Sticking in something like 'How to Bathe Your Cat' would clearly be bad marketing.
- You use the product yourself because, if you don't, you'll never know if you like it – and if that happens it will show through in your editorial and your readers will detect a lack of passion about the proposition.
- You endorse the product to your readership. Don't just send a sales letter to the subscriber list without first telling readers why you are enthusiastic about the product.

You'll have some planning and researching to accomplish before you attract endorsement income, but if you make the effort the rewards are substantial.

Do not be timid about approaching programme contractors on the subject of endorsement. Many of them consider it as effective as affiliate reselling.

11 – Promote revenue-sharing affiliate programmes

Another way to generate income from your e-zine is to use it to promote revenue-sharing affiliate programmes. You can usually join these free of charge, and all that will be required is that you provide a link to the appropriate Web site. This link will include a tracking code that uniquely identifies you as the affiliate that supplied the prospect. If the prospect bites, you will receive commission ranging from 5 to 50 per cent of the purchase price.

There are thousands of these programmes available on the Internet and, like joint ventures, it is good marketing practice to select those that most closely match the profile of your e-zine readership. You can locate a searchable directory of 3,136 such opportunities at this site:

http://www.AssociatePrograms.com

This is the obvious route to take when you don't trade with your own products, and it pays well.

What theme could you use for producing your own e-zine? There are many theme-based e-zines around. Here's a handful of ideas for your consideration:

■ *News.* You could provide timely, interesting and current news articles on a specific industry. To compile the background material, scan news items in your area of interest and summarize the content into snippets of information.
■ *Tip of the day.* These are short, concise tips on just about any topic: marketing, share dealing, money matters, National Lottery, betting, etc.
■ *Web site update.* If you don't have the time to publish a full-blown e-zine, you could send out regular weekly updates on what's happening at your Web site. Did someone post an interesting message on the discussion board? Have you published an interesting article?
■ *Special interest e-zine.* This is the most common type of e-zine. It contains articles, news, events and tips covering a specific topic or industry. Think of any topic and the odds are there is an e-zine or two (200 perhaps) currently published on that topic, but there is always room for more, providing you put your own unique twist on the subject.
■ *E-zine-based training classes.* Publish a lesson a week to teach others a particular skill: sales training, Internet marketing, software development, lead generation, Web design, etc. Use your accumulated knowledge and expertise to teach others and in the process you will attract a following of loyal subscribers.
■ *Web-based e-zines.* Instead of an e-mailed e-zine you could publish a weekly or monthly Web-based 'e-magazine'. This is more difficult to produce but it allows you to take full

Figure 4.2 Over 3,000 reseller opportunities available at this site
(**http://www.AssociatePrograms.com**)

advantage of the technology available to Web developers:
real audio and video, interactive discussion board and chat
rooms. Many technology e-zines incorporate this format.

▧ *Affiliate marketing.* If you have a product or service that you
sell through affiliates, you will definitely sell more through
this category of e-zine. Devoted to helping your affiliates sell
higher volumes of your product, an affiliate e-zine should
contain marketing strategies, tactics, tips and success stories
from your top producers. It can encourage the newcomers to
become more enterprising and profitable in their activities.

▧ *Cool site of the day.* Similar to the 'tip of the day' e-zine, you
basically surf the Web and locate interesting and note-
worthy sites within your particular niche. Then you write a
brief review and publish it, accompanied by relevant links.

▧ *Resources list.* Publish a list of resources in your field. What
types of software tools do you use? What equipment do you
use? Which sites do you visit? Keep a list of these and
publish them in a weekly e-zine.

▧ *Multi-step promotional e-zine.* Promote your product or
service to your opt-in lists with a regular, timed campaign of
e-mailed letters that both teach and sell.

If you create your own subscription-based Web site, you will present yourself with 10 opportunities to start a home-based Internet business. Once the domain of adult sites, subscription sites are quickly becoming mainstream. In particular, business and finance sites are embracing the 'pay-to-view' model because it allows them to concentrate their efforts on building a Web site that services a small group of paying visitors. These subscription-based operators are discovering that this is more cost-effective than endeavouring to profit from the casual surfer who jumps from one free site to another, devouring information without paying.

A subscription-based Web site charges a fee for access to the information and electronic tools on the site. After users pay the fee they are provided with a user ID and password that will enable them to access the site for a given period of time, usually either a month or a year. In the case of monthly access, the fee is normally set up to be automatically charged to the subscriber's credit card once a month. This is known as a 're-occurring' payment. The downside here though is that the subscriber may cancel at any time and avoid future charges. It is best to go for money up front on a yearly subscription basis.

The following 10 ideas are ways to make money on the Internet with 'pay-to-view' Web sites.

12 – Become a niche solution provider

Set yourself up as a 'complete solution' for a particular industry by offering software tools, lead generation tools, articles, etc for your designated market.

Examples include subscription sites for:

- estate agents;
- used car dealers;
- Internet marketers;
- insurance agents;
- advertising agents;
- writing circles;
- accountants;
- surveyors.

The Success Arsenal is a classic example of a subscription site that is exclusively devoted to providing how-to information to Internet marketers. Its breathtaking panorama of information and services comprises:

- e-mail account facilities;
- Web hosting;
- Web page creation tools;
- autoresponders;
- e-commerce instruction and tools;
- CGI (Common Gateway Interface) tools;
- press release service;
- networking;
- e-zines;
- mass mailing;
- classified ad pages;
- link pages;
- search engines;
- banner exchanges;
- submission software and services;
- over 1,000 affiliate reseller programmes.

Go now to the Success Arsenal Web site and see in how many ways you could link its structure to your own conception of a subscription-based Web site.

http://www.SuccessArsenal.com

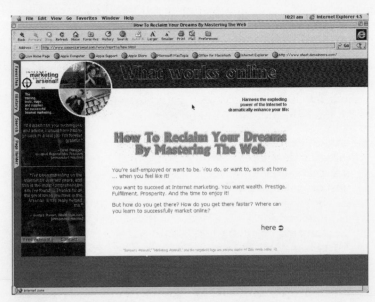

Figure 4.3 Example of a niche solution provider
(**http://www.SuccessArsenal.com**)

If you possess expert knowledge in any particular field of commercial activity, think seriously about setting yourself up as a niche solution provider on the Internet. Don't worry about provision of the necessary electronic tools – you'll locate them all somewhere or other for free in cyberspace.

13 – Set up a fee-based discussion board

Do you have a special topic about which you feel passionate, about which you'd like to share information with others? Then set up your own discussion board on the Internet and get paid for your efforts.

You could of course be altruistic and do it for no reward by joining the plethora of free discussion boards on just about any topic imaginable. However, the problem with free discussion boards is that by their very nature they are prone to abuse and offer limited value to participants. Indeed, most free discussion boards are no more than glorified spam factories. Unless they are constantly 'moderated', discussion boards become a place for promoters to place their affiliate-programme-of-the-day link.

On the other hand, recognized experts in the particular market you are targeting will moderate a paid-subscription-only discussion board. Participants would only be allowed to post messages and replies using their ID. Add to this the fact that all the participants have paid a fee and are therefore motivated, and you have the formula for a successful subscription-based discussion board.

Here are three examples of very active and very profitable paid discussion boards:

- *The Internet Marketing Challenge*. This is a discussion board for Internet marketers where, according to the home page, subscribers (for an annual fee of £155) can have access to a host of functions including:
    - Get your questions answered free of charge by high-paid Internet consultants, as often as you want (so you can stop spending hours or even days frustrated and hunting for answers).
    - Get your Web site or marketing campaign evaluated free of charge by these same high-paid experts (and find out instantly what's holding you back from Internet wealth).
    - Be privy to insider methods for starting, promoting and marketing your business, product or service on the

Internet, methods that are simple, risk-free and up-to-the-minute fresh.
http://www.Internetmarketingchallenge.com

- *The Universal Thread.* This is a discussion board for computer programming professionals, which charges a yearly fee of £60 for access.
http://www.universalthread.com

- *The Blackjack Review Network.* This one is dedicated to winning at blackjack! It charges £21 annually for access.
http://www.bjrnet.com

If you have a bee in your bonnet, set up a paid discussion board and get paid for allowing other people to let off steam. If you like people, if you like controversy, if you like discussion, this could be the home-based Internet business for you.

14 – Become an electronic tool provider

If you have the ability to develop Internet tools that could assist other users to perform tasks more easily or to simplify their

Figure 4.4   Example of a state-of-the-art electronic tool provider
(**http://ultimateadvertisingclub.com**)

lives, you have the basis for a profitable subscription-based Web site business.

The Ultimate Advertising Club is an example of a classic electronic tool provider. Most Web sites belong to the 99 per cent of sites that don't get enough targeted traffic to create any true and predictable flow of sales. This Web site is all about joining the 1 per cent of sites that get the traffic and make the sale. It's about getting the traffic and getting the order.

http://ultimateadvertisingclub.com

This one will work for you if you have the technical know-how to create and develop useful electronic tools.

15 – Open up your Web site as a training centre

This is a site that contains information and tools to help subscribers learn or enhance a particular skill. Online classes, real audio and video lessons, and teleclasses are a few of the features that you could offer.

BigPlayStocks is a good example. It's a training centre for investors, and offers its subscribers a variety of packages. It's worth a visit just to see what goes into planning a training centre Web site.

http://www.bigplaystocks.com

Are you a skilled trainer? Are you willing to share your accumulated knowledge with others? Do you have the technical ability? If so – on all three counts – then go for it. You will earn a very handsome income for your efforts.

16 – Create a resource centre and sell access to the list

Compile a list of resources that are employed in a particular industry and sell access to the list. There are several such subscription-based Web sites on the Internet right now, sites relating to government contracting assignments, domain names and classified ads.

Take an early look at one such successful resource centre that sells a list of free classified ad sites: Online Classified Club.

http://www.tunza-products.com/classified/ads.html

Cyberspace resource centres are becoming increasingly popular, and various categories of Internet users will subscribe to those sites that offer genuine resource lists.

17 – Develop methods for driving traffic to Web sites

Do you know an effective method of driving traffic to Web sites? Or could you develop a software tool that builds traffic? Such valuable information could be developed into a profitable subscription-based Web site business.

Link-O-Matic uses this idea effectively and profitably. Apart from allowing access to proven traffic-building tools, it also provides open discussion and support forums where marketing questions are answered by successful Webmasters, and

Figure 4.5 How to drive traffic to Web sites (**http://www.linkomatic.com**)

subscribers can share their experiences, show off their expertise, learn Internet marketing tips and tricks, or just start a general discussion. Link-O-Matic guarantees subscribers that every question will be answered.

http://www.linkomatic.com

This opportunity is for the skilled Webmaster exclusively. If that description fits you, then give this business some serious thought. There are millions of Web site owners out there who haven't a clue about how to attract users to their expensively designed Web sites.

18 – Create an exclusive e-zine article centre

E-zine publishing is an exploding industry, and the tens of thousands of e-zine publishers worldwide all have one thing in common – they need a constant flow of fresh content for their publications. Combine this with the fact that there is available to you an equally constant pool of writers who would love to have their articles published in exchange for a promotional link, and you have the potential for a great subscription-based Web site.

If you have a thirst for information and possess highly developed organizational skills, give serious consideration to this particular way of making money on the Internet. You do not need to be technically minded to create an e-zine article centre because there is ample free help available, right there on the Internet. If this opportunity appeals to you, go for it, because not too many people are doing it yet.

19 – Charge a fee for receiving your e-zine

If you can offer absolutely the best information available for a particular industry you can charge a fee for your e-zine. However (because there are already many free e-zines around on the Internet), to be successful you will need to offer your prospects added value by piling on free bonuses for subscribing.

Here is an example of one e-zine that does all of that and in the process attracts subscriptions of £12.50 per month from authors, publishers, self-publishers, speakers, book promoters, consultants, coaches and trainers. This e-zine, entitled *Sell Your Brain Food*, promises to reveal the secrets for successfully promoting and selling 10,000 or more copies of any printed book, e-book, audiotape, videotape or newsletter, these secrets purportedly emanating from authors and experts who are already doing it.

http://www.sellyourbrainfood.com

You've just read how one operator does it. Could you create an e-zine of such interest that Internet users would gladly pay a subscription to receive it?

20 – Charge fees for access to your referrals directory

How's this for an idea? Offer homeowners access to a directory of reliable, recommended contractors, plumbers, electricians, painters, landscapers, etc, and charge a fee for access to your exclusive directory.

Angie's List is a consumer-driven organization that collects customer satisfaction ratings on local service companies in more than 250 categories. This referrals directory offers assistance to subscribers on a wide range of areas of interest to homeowners.

http://www.angieslist.com

Here is a small selection from the list, which was originally compiled by one woman based in the Midwest of the United States:

accounting	appliance repair
air duct cleaning	appliance sales
alarm companies	appraisals
alterations	architect services
animal grooming	artist services
animal kennels	asbestos removal
animal removal	auctions
animal training	auto alarms
antique shops	auto bodywork

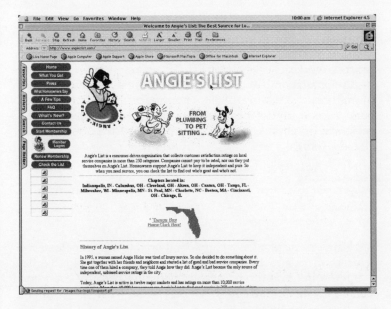

Figure 4.6 Angie's List: the Web's number one referrals directory
(**http://www.angieslist.com**)

auto dealerships
auto glass
auto inspections
auto oil change
auto painting
auto radio service
auto retailing
auto service
auto tyres
auto towing
awnings

barber services
basement waterproofing
basketball goals
bathtubs
bicycles
billiard table sales
blind cleaning
boat service/repair
bookkeeping

bridal shops
buffing and polishing

cabinetmaking
cake decorating
calligraphy
camcorder repair
camera repair
carpenters
carpet cleaning
carpet dyeing
carpet installation
car washes
catering
cellular phone
ceramic tile
chef services
chimney cleaning
clock repair
closet remodelling
clowns

computer repair	excavating
computer sales	exercise equipment
computer training	exterminating
concrete work	
costume rental	florist
countertops	framing
	furnace vacuuming
decks and porches	furniture, custom
delivery service	furniture repair and
disc jockeys	refinishing
dock building	furniture sales
doors	
drainpipes	garage doors

You learnt in Chapter 2 how my friend used this concept to nego-tiate fees on his subscription-based Web site for nationwide B & Bs.

Internet referral directories are booming because everyone wants a one-stop source for what they want, when they want it, which is invariably right now.

21 – Provide an information-on-demand service

The final thought in this section is to set up a subscription-based Web site business to provide fast access to timely data for a desig-nated industry, market sector or sub-sector. Companies and commercial institutions that rely on accurate, timely data are willing to pay handsomely for access to a site that guarantees up-to-date, accurate information. Examples include stock, bond and commodity quotes, government contract bid requests, mortgage rates, pending legislation and government statistics.

Provision of accurate timely information is what the Internet is really all about. If you can provide such information on demand, you will make money.

The following sections consider seven businesses that offer high-profit services to the Internet community. Are you a Webmaster or are you in the process of attaining that status? Could you provide a specific service to other Webmasters that would save them time or money? Or can you help other businesses establish a Web presence? If so, you have the basis for a profitable service-based Internet business.

Even if you don't possess the skills required, you could quickly learn them on the Internet, and usually at no cost. Most service providers start off in this way. They have an interest in some aspect of Web development or marketing, and find resources on the Internet that teach them how to provide these services.

The following sections are devoted to signalling a few of the services you can offer, together with some resources that teach you how to provide these services to others.

22 – Become a CGI script installer

CGI (Common Gateway Interface) is the most popular programming language used to build interactive Web sites. If you have ever signed a Web site's guestbook, participated in a discussion forum, placed a classified ad or used just about any other tool on a Web site, then you have witnessed at first hand what CGI can do.

A CGI programme is more commonly known as a script: a series of instructions that tell the server what to do and then bring the results back to the browser to display. For example, if you are using a search tool on a Web site, you enter the word or phrase into the entry field and hit the 'find' or 'submit' button. This action then invokes a CGI script that looks for occurrences of your search term in an index on the server. The CGI script retrieves the matches from the server and brings them back for the browser to display. All this takes place in just a few seconds.

A CGI script installer doesn't actually write the CGI programmes but rather installs existing scripts on the client's server. So where do you find these existing CGI programmes? There are several libraries available online offering hundreds of free CGI scripts. The following one is among the best:

http://www.cgi-resources.com

Here is a partial list of the Web site content:

- *Remotely hosted* (440 files). Can't run your own CGI applications? Get them hosted for you remotely!
- *Documentation* (130 files). Information, documentation and tutorials regarding CGI programming.
- *Books* (18 titles). Books related to the various topics found in CGI programming.

▓ *Programmers* (32 files). Lists freelance CGI programmers and companies to solve your problems.

The best way to approach this business

Read up on the CGI language because, even though you do not need to write the programs, as an installer you should be familiar with how they work. Understanding the interworkings will help you get up to speed on doing the installations and assist you to troubleshoot problems. Go to the following site for a great tutorial:

http://www.cgi101.com

Even newcomers to the Internet can get up to speed quickly through diligent application to the intensive instruction and tools available from cgi-resources.com.

23 – Offer an electronic press release service

This is a service where you fax a client's press release to targeted members of the media. The Internet Marketing Warriors offer their members a free database of over 7,000 fax numbers and e-mail addresses of core global media. If you are interested, go to the following site for membership information:

http://www.thewarriorgroup.com

For further information on this particular way of making money on the Internet, you might also want to visit the following Web site, which offers a completely integrated one-stop press release service:

http://www.press-releases.net

If this way of making money on the Internet interests you, you'll find all the necessary tools at the two Web sites listed. Spend some time at both sites, choose the one you feel most comfortable with, sign up and make a start on your new home-based Internet business.

24 – Learn how to create a search engine positioning service

In estate agency practice, the most important aspect of the marketing strategy is location, location, location. The Internet equivalent to this adage is *position, position and position*. A search engine positioning service helps clients get their Web sites listed within the top of the search engine results. This higher-than-average positioning almost guarantees high traffic for the site. Operators of this type of service keep up with the latest tools and techniques for top Web site positioning, and employ these resources to build doorway pages that rank high on the search engine indexes.

You can find out more about search engine placement by visiting the following site:

http://www.searchengineforums.com/bin/Ultimate.cgi

There is a learning curve required to take advantage of this opportunity, but your application in mastering the skills will pay off handsomely because the demand for the service is huge – and growing.

25 – Operate a key phrase discovery service

This service examines a Web site and produces a list of all the keywords and keyword phrases that are relevant to the site's content. This keyword list can then be used to:

■ build keyword-specific doorway pages for search engine submission;
■ advertise on pay-for-click services such as Goto.com and FindWhat.com;
■ find link partners;
■ find targeted advertising media.

The GoTo keyword search tool is of tremendous assistance in locating keywords. This resource lists the number of searches on the site for a particular keyword during the previous month.

http://www.goto.com/d/about/advertisers/faq.jhtml

This is another business that requires some application on your part before you get going, but the information and tools you need are all available, just waiting for you to pull down and get started on a money-making venture.

26 – Earn money with your own classified ad submission centre

There are literally thousands of free classified ad sites on the Internet but the problem with some of these sites is that they have limited traffic, and so using them individually as promotional tools is basically a hit-or-miss proposition.

What is not generally known is that there is software available that will allow you to submit automatically to hundreds of classified sites at a time. This greatly increases your chances of getting traffic.

One way to profit from this situation is to purchase the classified submission software and then offer to submit clients' ads for a fee. You could charge £25–£35 to submit an ad every week for a month to 200–300 sites.

The software you need to operate this business is available at the following site:

http://www.becanada.com/

This one is simple. It will cost you a little money to start off with, but the hours are short and you can accumulate substantial income in a market that is booming.

27 – Offer a Web site design service

If you possess (or have the desire to learn) the HTML skills necessary, you can build Web sites for businesses looking to establish a Web presence. For several years now, business owners have been hearing on the news and reading in the press that if they don't get around to doing business on the Internet they will be out of business. The problem here is that the majority have no idea how to build a Web site for themselves. Add to this the fact that the investment required to hire a specialist house to create a custom Web site is quite out of the reach of most small businesses.

As an independent operator in your own home-based business, you could offer an inexpensive but lucrative solution by providing a template-based Web site. What you do is put together a sample Web site complete with navigation, guestbook, discussion board and 5–10 blank pages that will be used to fill in information and illustrations about local businesses. Using this simple template, take atmospheric pictures of actual local businesses (storefronts are fine) and insert a picture of each of these businesses on a separate Web page. Then contact each business owner in turn and demonstrate what his or her business would look like on the Internet. Offer to insert additional pictures and information about services and products. Charge a minimum fee, say £300, for the Web design. In addition charge a hosting fee of £15–£30 per month.

For free CGI scripts (guestbooks, discussion boards, etc) visit the following site:

http://www.cgi-resources.com

For details on Web hosting services go to the following site:

http://www.pair.com

You can negotiate with Pair.com to obtain virtual domain hosting for £1 per month, providing you have a Webmaster account with them. Doing it in this way, clients have their own domain name – **www.whatever.com** – which would be hosted under your Webmaster account. Assuming you charged £15 per month for hosting, you would be taking £14 profit per month from every site you host!

This is another excellent fee-based opportunity. All you need to know is available at the sites listed.

28 – Set up as a Web graphics designer/ copywriter

Let's look first at the copywriting aspect. A Web site's copy and how it is laid out can make all the difference between a profitable site and one that simply exists and costs money to maintain. You can charge substantial amounts if you can compose copy that sells.

For information on Web copywriting visit the following site:

http://www.write101.com

Do you have a talent for drawing or graphics design?

If so, you can make a good living creating graphic content and artwork for Web sites. To solicit business, surf the Web and find commercial sites that could use a graphics makeover. Contact the Webmaster (whose address is usually featured on the home page) and offer your services.

Proficient writers and designers are always in demand on the Internet. If you are good, word will spread fast and you could end up with more work than you can handle. Should you be so lucky, go out and hire someone equally talented to assist in the servicing of your increased workload.

The following ideas suggest how you can profit from the software industry (even if you can't programme). Don't skip over this short section just because you are not a software developer or programmer. You can make money in the software development industry without writing a single line of code.

Alternatively, if you *are* a programmer, the ideas featured here might give you fresh insight on how to channel your skills – and if you ever wanted to be a software developer but never got around to it, this may now be the best time to start learning. The development tools available on the Internet allow you to build applications using simple point-and-click interfaces with very little coding required. So no matter which category you fit into, check out these ideas. You may not become the next Bill Gates. But then again, who knows?

29 – Develop a desktop application

If you do possess the necessary skills you could develop applications that people can download direct from the Internet. The model for this business is to create the application with a 30- to 60-day timed limit. That way your prospects may download and test-run the software. If they like it, they can then purchase from you a code that registers the software and terminates the timed limit.

To obtain some ideas on the types of software to develop, visit discussion boards specializing in your particular area of interest. Pay attention to the various problems for which people are seeking solutions, and then develop software that provides ideal solutions.

30 – Become an application service provider

Application service providers host Web-based applications on their Web sites and charge people an appropriate fee for usage. This is a very exciting way to make money on the Internet, and experts forecast that within the next few years just about every desktop application will be Web-based. For complete information visit the following site:

http://www.aspnews.com/

Anyone can learn how to become an ASP. The provision of application services as a way to make money on the Internet shows huge potential for years to come.

31 – Develop an industry-specific spreadsheet template

You don't need to be a programmer to develop a spreadsheet template. Simply write a pre-formatted spreadsheet that can be used for a specific industry. For example, in the financial industry, write spreadsheets that calculate mortgage amortization schedules or prepayment models, or write a whole suite of plug-and-play templates and offer them as a package.

This one could be operated in tandem with several others from the opportunities listed in this section.

32 – Write custom CGI scripts

Earlier in the chapter we talked about providing a CGI script installation service. With just a little more expertise you could write and sell your own CGI scripts. Writing CGI scripts is much easier than you think. The following site has a very good, easy-to-follow tutorial:

http://www.cgi101.com

You could either write CGI scripts on spec for Webmasters who have a specific requirement, or you could write several off-the-shelf scripts and offer them from your Web site.

An example of a site that sells several niche CGI scripts is given below:

http://www.cgi-resources.com/

If you learn how to write CGI scripts and couple that skill with offering an installation service, you could have the beginnings of a profitable home-based Internet business.

33 – Develop a database of useful information

Put together a database of related information and sell access to it on the Internet, or package the information as a database application. The database doesn't have to be complicated. It can be as simple as a Web site that has an alphabetical list of classified ad sites to which you sell access.

If you can compile information that is needed by a certain niche market, you will be able to charge for the privilege of accessing the data.

A database or collection of related information can be stored and accessed directly from the Internet. You sell access to the database interface that allows the user to search for the specific information required.

Here are some examples of databases that you could set up on the Internet:

- *E-zine database.* Compile a list of e-zines that sell classified ads. Include information such as number of subscribers, ad cost, frequency, etc. You can sell access to this information to marketers who are looking for targeted places to advertise. For an example of this concept, see *The Directory of Ezines*: **http://www.lifestylespub.com/clickbank/?hop=jjjones/ lifestyles**
- *Media contacts for press releases.* Similar to the e-zine database, you could compile a list of core media contacts, and this information could be sold to marketers who wish to send press releases to targeted media.
- *Newspaper advertising database.* A list of all the European daily and weekly newspapers along with their classified ad rates, circulation, readership, etc.
- *Magazine advertising database.* Similar list of magazines that accept classified ads.

■ *CV database.* Allow job hunters the opportunity to post their CVs in your database and charge employers to access and search the CVs from the Internet. The best way to approach this is to target a specific industry, such as computing, advertising or accounting.

■ *Industry-specific database.* Every industry has a need for specific information in a searchable format. Look at your own field of expertise and establish whether you can identify a specific need for compilation.

■ *Employment database.* Compile a list of jobs available for a particular industry. Sell access to job hunters.

■ *Sports stats.* Compile a list of sports-related information for use by fantasy sports players.

You don't have the technical skill to develop your own software products?

Not a problem. Many software products offer affiliate reseller programmes that allow you to earn commission by marketing the software. Here are a few:

http://www.anaconda.net/
http://www.AffiliateTracking.com/
http://www.animfactory.com/affiliate.html
http://www.oska.com/tahni.pht

Of all the software opportunities featured in this section, compiling databases has the greatest potential. On the other hand, you could opt to sell custom-made databases as an affiliate reseller and earn substantial monthly commission.

34 – Offer cyberspace training and coaching

When Prime Minister Tony Blair announced that he wanted the Internet to be available to everyone, training and coaching featured strongly among the benefits he envisaged for the populace at large. Now commercial users worldwide are fast discovering the advantages the Internet affords to facilitating coaching and training through interactive Web sites, real audio and video, and software products.

Here how to exploit this exploding opportunity:

- *CGI programming tutorials.* If you know CGI programming you can develop online tutorials that teach others how to write programs. You then have the choice of either selling access to the tutorials or offering them for free but selling more advanced courses. For an example of this, visit the following Web site:
  http://www.cgi101.com
- *Web connectivity tutorials.* There's a lot involved for anyone in getting their first Web site connected on the Internet. If you have the skills to put it all together, people will pay to have a step-by-step guide (book, CD ROM, video) that shows exactly what to do and which software to use.
- *Java tutorials.* Java is the programming language to use for developing database applications on the Internet. It allows for much more flexibility, speed and bandwidth than does CGI. However, as Java is much more difficult to master than CGI, it would be best to approach this business by catering for software programmers who want to learn how to leverage their skills on the Web. For example, you could create tutorials that show programmers how to establish database connectivity to Web sites.
- *Lead generation coaching.* As long as there are salespeople, there will be a demand for prospect leads, and if you can teach sellers how to generate more leads, they will beat a path to your door to get at your skills training products. The key is to specialize in one specific industry; you can choose from estate agents, car dealers, stockbrokers, mortgage lenders, financial advisers, etc. What you could do is create a Web site that gives them some free information and then sell them more advanced courses in the form of videos or how-to manuals. Visit the following Web site to see how it's done:
  http://www.leads4insurance.com/
- *Internet marketing tutorial.* There are any number of Internet marketing courses on offer and the majority of these are in the form of manuals that are downloadable. Is there perhaps an opening here for a multi-video format? This animated approach could take viewers from A to Z and show them how to develop and market a Web site. It could also demonstrate how to use software tools, where to advertise and how to install simple CGI scripts to boost traffic.
- *Sales coaching.* Unlike lead generation coaching, sales coaching does not necessarily require to be targeted to a

specific market but can teach sales techniques in general to a wide variety of sales professionals.

■ *Weight-loss coaching.* Develop a Web site devoted to helping people lose weight and you're on your way to creating a successful home-based Internet business. One way to approach this opportunity is to create a referral centre to assist users to find partners in their quest to lose weight. Then you go on to sell participants weight-loss videos, menus, menu planning or even weekly teleclasses.

■ *Health and fitness coaching.* Similar to weight-loss coaching, this concept could be adapted to helping people to get in shape. Offer videos and manuals on exercise, weight lifting, nutrition, etc.

■ *Online golf coaching.* Help golfers improve their game by offering free tips on driving, putting, posture, etc, and then sell them videos, manuals and teleclasses.

If you are an experienced programmer, training and coaching is where the money is.

35 – Develop a vortal

A vortal – or vertical portal – is a Web site that provides a one-stop gateway to other Web sites with the same theme. Think of a vortal as a combination of a portal and theme Web site.

A portal (such as Yahoo or AltaVista) provides a gateway through which you can reach sites covering a wide range of topics. Conversely, a vortal concentrates on one specific topic and covers that topic in as much depth as is conceivable. However, unlike a theme site, it does not provide its own content. A vortal can be as simple as a list of topics and content with links to the originating Web sites.

To operate a vortal successfully you need to find (and link to) interesting and informative sites within your theme and, of course, you must also drive a steady stream of traffic to your site. You can make money with a vortal by either selling advertising or selling your own products related to the theme of the site.

Here are some ideas for vortal sites:

■ pets and animals;
■ food and recipes;

- business opportunities;
- health and fitness;
- sports;
- automotive;
- gardening;
- Web development;
- Internet marketing;
- employment.

Not everyone's cup of tea and a lot of hard work involved here, but you can make money on a regular basis out of creating and operating a vortal as a home-based business venture.

five

Creating **your**
master plan

Hopefully by now you are settling on an idea for the Internet business you intend to start at home and here is where you start to piece together your master plan for achievement. Even if you are as yet undecided and making up your mind between two or three alternatives, still crack on, adding flesh to the bones of the outline you have already created. Leave the sections on competition, packaging, marketing and selling on the Internet until you have completed your first reading of the book, but start now on the other sections.

Plan ahead for success

Don't be put off if you've never written a business plan before. You have an idea, you want to start a business, and what you're about to do now is to slot into position all the nuts and bolts to create a plan of action that will transform your idea into a practical reality. Do not consider the construction of the plan as a chore. It should be fun, and as it develops so too will inspiration as your creative juices begin to flow freely.

The initial purpose is to keep you focused on all matters relevant to the successful launch of your enterprise, but there is another equally valid reason for creating and developing your master plan. Even now you should be thinking ahead and planning for the future. You won't need much if anything in the way of start-up funding but the day may come when you require to submit your plan to external sources for expansion purposes.

Plan now for that eventuality, so that if or when that day arrives you will be in a position to take instant action. Work on your plan consistently; make it a part of your everyday routine. If you don't take it that seriously, one day you might find yourself scrabbling around and cobbling together words and numbers that fall short of the mark as a persuasive instrument in your quest for financial assistance.

Make sure the plan has your imprint

Whatever the format of your final draft, make sure it's got your hand on it. You may need some help with the structure, but if you follow the guidelines provided in this chapter you won't go far wrong. Do not be tempted (even if you have the money) to assign this essential work to a consultant. This is your dream and, to convert it into reality, it is you who has to see it through.

Just remember, it's not the size of the plan that matters but what goes into it. Keep the document brief, succinct and to the point. Do it this way and you'll discover that a handful of A4 pages will suffice.

Choosing an effective Internet trading name

There's a lot in a name but even more in a trading name. You should make a start on developing a suitable name for your enterprise by listing as many ideas as you can come up with. Getting it right from the start is crucial because you don't want to be obliged to change it after a few months of trading. There are a few house rules to observe and ideally your trading name should meet these requirements:

■ Keep to a maximum of nine letters in the composition of the core word (preferably less).
■ Keep to a maximum of three syllables in its pronunciation (preferably two).
■ The name must look and sound right.
■ It should fit the purpose of the enterprise.

■ It should be apposite to the marketplace.
■ It must be acceptable for use on the Internet.

Composition

The crisper the trading name, the more memorable it will be. Consider the composition and the number of letters in each of these famous Internet names: Microsoft (9), Hotmail (7), Yahoo (5), Freeserve (9), Netscape (8). Keep it short and simple and, providing it complies with the other guidelines, your name will work for you.

Two or three syllables

Good names are simple to pronounce; they just roll off the tongue because of fewer syllables, for example Shock-wave (2), Hot-send (2), Cor-el (2), Pri-max (2) and the famous names above, Mi-cro-soft (3), Hot-mail (2), Ya-hoo (2), Free-serve (2), Net-scape (2). Avoid tongue twisters at all costs.

Looking and sounding right

If you get the first two guidelines right your trading name will sound OK, but it also has to look good for graphic development in such a visible medium as the Internet. That's why single word names work best as a rule. Even so, you can sometimes cheat a little and get away with it by butting three words together as one in the form of an Internet graphic, for example JimsWebStore.

Fitting the purpose

This seems pretty obvious. However, you'll encounter a host of inappropriate trading names in cyberspace. Take good care at the start and avoid this pitfall.

Suiting the marketplace

Your marketplace is the Internet, so endeavour to inject a hint of high tech in the composition of your chosen name.

Acceptable for use on the Internet

Before your logo becomes established, make sure you can use it as the domain name for your Web site. Once you have made up your mind on a suitable name, endeavour to register it with InterNIC. If it has already been taken, you'll have to try again – and that is why it's best to have a few alternatives to choose from.

Defining your business status

Unless your idea has incredible potential you will almost certainly start out as a sole trader in your home-based Internet business. Just be conscious of what this entails: should your enterprise fail you will be personally liable for all debts incurred.

Allow for taxation

This is not a subject we need delve into in detail this early in your adventure, but it would be prudent to make some allowance for its ensuing inevitability. You should be thinking in terms of:

- income tax;
- National Insurance contributions (NIC);
- value added tax (VAT) in the fullness of time.

Preparing your accounts

Should your business turnover (total sales) before expenses fall below £15,000 for a full year of trading, you will not be required to provide detailed accounts. Instead, a simple three-line summary will suffice, for example:

Turnover	£14,657
Less purchases and expenses	£5,500
Net profits	£9,157

Creating the blueprint

This is where you discover whether or not you *really and truly* want to start an Internet business at home. Get it all down on paper: the good, the bad and the ugly. Omit nothing or you will live to regret it once you are under way. Let your head rule your heart in the execution of your blueprint and you will become the architect of your own success.

Formulate your blueprint under the following headings:

- *Executive summary*
  - Brief description of the idea behind your business.
  - Target market.
  - Unique aspects (if any).
- *Management expertise*
  - How much you already know about Internet marketing.
  - How much you know about your product or service.
  - List the skills you still have to acquire.
- *The concept*
  - Just what is your idea?
  - Is it yours or does it emanate from another source?
  - Explain it briefly.
  - If it's brand-new, prove its practicality for Internet application.
  - If it has been around for years, who else is doing it on the Internet?
  - What's different about the idea?
  - Have you located a gap in the market?
- *Objectives*
  - List the objectives for your enterprise, short- and long-term.
  - Now show how you intend to realize these objectives.
- *Competition*
  - Do you know who your main competitors are in the global marketplace?
  - Detail their product ranges and illustrate where their ranges differ from yours.
  - If they are superior, say so; if they're not, explain why not.
  - If you perceive a gap in the market for your particular product or service, make a guess at how you think the competition will react on your entry into the marketplace.

■ *Product or service*
   - Devote one concise page to its description.
   - If it differs from competitive alternatives, say so.
   - If it's superior, say so.
   - If it's inferior, say so, and then explain why you believe it is still viable.
   - List the benefits to the end-user.
■ *Packaging the proposition*
   - Wrap your product or service into the benefits package you'll be offering your customers. Bear in mind that one difference makes all the difference.
   - Will it be discounting?
   - Will it be incentive marketing?
   - Will it be added-value service?
■ *Marketing your business on the Internet*
   - Keep your marketing strategy simple and relevant to the proposition.
   - How will you go about attracting visitors to your Web site?
   - Will you be using e-mail marketing?
   - Would you consider approaching user groups?
   - Will you be offering a free trial period?
   - Can you offer a choice of ways to pay?
   - Will you use free reports as an incentive to purchase?
   - Will you develop and circulate your own e-zine over the Internet?
   - Would you consider developing a promotional CD ROM?
■ *Selling on the Internet*
   - Your marketing strategy will determine the sales policy.
   - Are you confident in your ability to compose compelling sales messages?
   - If not, how do you intend to remedy this essential skill shortfall?
   - Do you know yet how to negotiate with faceless prospects?
   - How will you bring yourself up to speed on Internet selling?
■ *Production expenses*
   - List the costs of any extra tools you may require apart from the freebies you will locate on the Internet.
   - List the costs of any special applications you might need for your particular type of operation.

■ *Strengths and weaknesses*
You will already be familiar with upside elements in your projected enterprise. Now list the downside before someone else does it for you. No matter how brilliant your plan may appear, there are bound to be some weaknesses. List them and state how you intend to accommodate them.

■ *Financial projections*
   – Profit and loss for the first year of trading.
   – Cash flow for the period.
   – Balance sheet.

■ *Appendix*
   – CV.
   – Include anything else that doesn't seem to fit in elsewhere.

Steps and stairs to creating your master plan

■ Think of your master plan as a rolling document. When you complete the first draft, you just keep on adding to it as you progress in your new business.

■ Take your own counsel to ensure that the input is all of your own devising.

■ Consider several alternatives before selecting the trading name you'll run with.

■ Be aware of the implications of operating as a sole trader.

■ Make some provision for the inevitability of taxation.

Exercise

Start now on your blueprint for success. Take everything you've learnt so far on launching an Internet business at home and lay it all out into an initial master plan for achievement.

Locating **the freeware to build your business**

There is an amazing range of promotional software on the Internet and it's all available for instant download as shareware or freeware. You are not required to do *anything* to qualify and it's all there just waiting to be downloaded into your computer. In this chapter we will review an extensive collection, but our focus will in the main be centred on freeware products.

Shareware and freeware

When you download shareware you will normally be required to pay a small one-off fee that allows you to share the software with other users; with freeware you download the produce for free and it's yours to use for evermore.

How come they can just give the stuff away?

Manufacturers who classify their products as freeware do so for these purposes:

■ sponsorship;
■ advertising;
■ testing.

The promoters rake in a fortune in sponsorship and advertising rights, and the recipients (you included) become the market-place for product testing. Win–win all around.

How and where to locate the freebies

Literally hundreds of disparate electronic application product categories are available as shareware or freeware, but it could take the rest of your life to track them down if you didn't know where to look. You won't have to endure that because now I will show you how to locate the freebies.

You'll need unlimited e-mail facilities

As your enterprise gathers momentum, you would be well advised to apply for as many e-mail facilities as you can locate. You will need them to spread the flow of your incoming messages from sundry quarters. The good news is that you won't have to search for them because below is a list of 22 such facilities, all of which you can join for free.

You can have as many free e-mail addresses as you want

Sorting out and keeping track of responses to your promotional activities becomes easier when you have several e-mail addresses at your disposal. It's a good practice to allocate separate e-mail addresses for individual advertisements to ensure that the source of response is accurately identified. This is not a problem because you can have as many free e-mail addresses as you want.

Extra facilities save cluttering up your mailbox

You will receive hundreds of e-mail confirmations in response to your ads and many of these will be trying to sell *you* something else. There is no way around this but you can divert these confir-mations to alternative addresses to save cluttering up your main mailbox. Do not delete confirmations without checking them first – there could be gems of opportunity nestling among them.

Most of the accounts you choose will be Web-based

What this means is that you will be able to access your e-mail from any computer – a decided bonus when you are out and about on business or on holiday. Just pop into an Internet café and your incoming e-mails are all there, waiting to be checked over.

Learn to use e-mail efficiently

You need all the help you can get in your early days of e-mail marketing. If you haven't already done so, go now and download the latest version of Netscape Communicator for free. Its help section has one of the easiest tutorials to follow on learning how to use e-mail efficiently. Print out the pages and use them for reference.

These are 22 e-mail facilities you can join for free:

- http://conk.com
- http://hotmail.com
- http://www.themail.com
- http://lycos.com
- http://mailcity.com
- http://excite.com
- http://netaddress.usa.net
- http://www.yahoo.co.uk
- http://eudoramail.com
- http://postmaster.co.uk
- http://onlymail.com
- http://thedorm.com
- http://hempseed.com
- http://juno.com
- http://www.uk2.net
- http://netscape.net
- http://theglobe.com
- http://www.bizland.com
- http://nightmail.com
- http://www.bigfoot.com
- http://www.affiliatesupport.com/ascmail.htm
- http://www.teamon.com

TeamOn controls all of your group workings

This is a brand-new piece of electronic wizardry that allows you to house all of your e-mail requirements for groups and down-lines in a single convenient programme. You can sign up for free and it won't cost you a penny to use any or all of TeamOn's state-of-the-art facilities:

- Set yourself up as team leader.
- Create your own exclusive e-mail address, eg jim@wealth-wizard.teamon.com.
- Tag on addresses for team members, eg anita@wealth-wizard.teamon.com.

Here's some of what you get for free:

- an individual incoming and outgoing mail service for every team member;
- the creation of complete facilities for teams of up to 10;
- the creation of sub-user group facilities;
- autoresponders;
- secure servers for interchange of sensitive information;
- electronic work charts;
- a group calendar.

http://www.teamon.com

No need to pay for ad submission tools

Submission tools are simply the software used by Networkers in the transmission of promotional messages (such as e-mails, ads, e-zines) to prospects in cyberspace. In other words they are bulk mailers. You can download and try out these tools for free (and keep them), whereas if you were to purchase them in the open market you would get very little change back out of £1,000. Right now you may think you won't need all of them, but I can tell you from practical experience you will. Locate and download these goodies over the next few days and test them out over several weeks until you become acquainted with their individual facilities:

- *Spider*. Submit your URLs to an amalgam of 941 assorted sources: major and minor search engines, free-for-all (FFA)

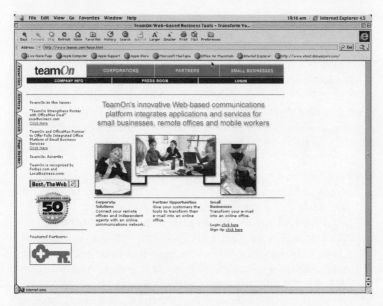

Figure 6.1 TeamOn houses multiple e-mail requirements
(**http://www.teamon.com**)

pages and classified ad sites. Incredibly fast submission to all sites in a single application takes six or seven minutes, and you get a detailed submission report on performance. You'll have to settle for fewer hits on the free no-time-limit trial, but a modest one-time payment gives you access to all 941 sites. Spider is a must for serious home-based business operators.
http://www.BizWeb2000.com

Ultimate Ad Tracker. Now here's a tool that acts as your personal researcher. The Ultimate Ad Tracker is perfect for the serious Networker who wants to know which ads work and which don't. It has 10 unique features:

- tracks hits by using different URLs for each ad campaign;
- tracks hits from any site to which you send traffic (eg affiliate programmes);
- password-protected admin area;
- shows all referring URLs;
- tracks total hits *and* total unique hits;
- all hits logged in an easy-to-read graphical format;
- tracks hits and unique hits by month, day or even down to the hour;

- better file-locking to handle much heavier loads;
- ability to edit all accounts;
- shows ratio of unique hits to total hits.

There is a free trial download.
http://www.thewarriorgroup.com/utrack.zip

Spend some time on the search engines to identify free download sources for the tools listed below. Use keywords such as 'Internet tools – FFA Blaster':

- *FFA Blaster*. The Blaster transmits your URLs to 1,000 FFA pages in minutes, and you may use the service as often as you wish. Get yours on a free-trial basis.
- *Classify98*. This is an essential piece of software for Networkers who regularly post ads to classified sites. Classify98 reaches 1,500 of them in just one quick posting. Available on free trial with limited sites run. Minimal one-off payment allows access to all 1,500 sites.
- *DHSC free submit*. Beams out your URLs to hundreds of search engines.
- *Classified Connection*. Connects to thousands of classified ad Web sites.
- *IMC tools*. Just about everything you'll ever need for electronic marketing.
- *Aureate group mailer*. Blasts out e-mails to groups.
- *Zenith bulk mailer*. Ditto.
- *Ad Wizard*. Files and categorizes all your promotional ads.
- *AdsPull*. Tells you how to write copy that sells.

Add these useful gizmos to your list:

- *Dump Truck*. Where to dump all those computer files no longer required.
- *Sobiz*. Helpful tools to get your business up and running.
- *Mti*. Electronic tool for transferring information rapidly.
- *NetContact*. Helps speed up Internet connection.
- *Stealth*. Provides useful tips on e-marketing.
- *Wise Wolf*. Sorts out classified ad files.

And now five amazing Internet communication tools available initially on a test market basis, and then yours to keep thereafter. Don't pass these by:

- *ICQ*. Talk to anyone anywhere direct from your computer and for free.
- *Adobe Micro Reader*. Downloads and lets you read and print out pdf files.
- *Hotsend*. Sends bulky files (such as this book) as a single attachment in a single e-mail.
- *Gator*. Fills in online forms automatically.
- *Shockwave*. Reaches parts of the Internet no other tool can.

You won't find it difficult to locate any of the above (and I don't want to make your induction too easy) if you apply yourself to regular, diligent search sessions.

Figure 6.2 Hotsend transmits bulky files all over the globe in seconds at the touch of a button (**http://hotsend.com**)

Choose the best autoresponder you can find

There are available to you literally hundreds of sources for free autoresponders (virtual office suites, for example) and I am not going to direct you to any one source in particular. Do your own search so that you can get a feel for what's on offer. Just ensure that the autoresponder of your choice has the entire range of features listed below:

- *Immediate autoresponse.* The facility to ensure that the very first message you send out to enquirers can be as long or as short as you wish.
- *Follow-ups.* You may issue unlimited follow-ups, but seven is the accepted maximum in Internet circles. If they haven't bitten after the seventh approach, you're wasting your time.
- *Edit suites.* These allow you to freshen up or completely change the copy for both immediate messages and follow-ups.
- *Test facility.* Send yourself test messages as a precaution prior to submission.
- *Opt-in list.* All incoming enquiries are catalogued (names and e-mail addresses) into a convenient list that in time will build up to form your own exclusive safe prospects list.
- *Add/remove.* This facility enables you to manually add and remove unwanted enquirers.

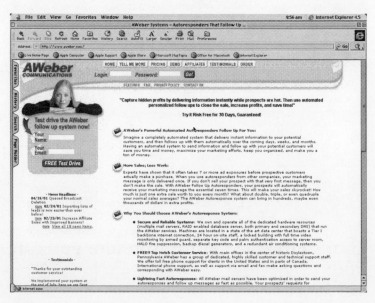

Figure 6.3 AWeber: one of the best autoresponders available on the Internet (**http://www.aweber.com**)

■ *E-mail*. You can send one-off messages on unrelated topics to your entire aggregated following.

How do you find all this free stuff?

As a matter of fact, I didn't find any of them, not one. *They just came to me*. The Internet loves winners and it loves triers almost as much. When it sees you give it your best shot, it simply reaches out and gratuitously throws things at you to help you on your way. It will happen to you too if you always give it your best shot. You'll be offered more and better stuff because Internet technology progresses at the speed of light and it's the *triers* who are invited to test-market (and keep) the industry's newest inventions.

Making sure you put it all to best use

First off: locate and then download those freebies for which you think you have an immediate requirement. Log the remainder in your 'accumulated information' file for future use. Do this now, and then start using your immediate tools on a regular basis. Some may seem strange at first but persist and the best computer of all (your brain) will very soon effect complete mastery over them.

Steps and stairs to selecting electronic tools

■ Freeware helps you build your business without incurring cost.
■ Take advantage of all free tools to complement your own endeavours.
■ When you use these tools, both you and the developers prosper.
■ Sign up for several e-mail facilities. You'll need them in time.

Exercise

One evening this week, spend an hour or so searching the Internet for as many items of shareware and freeware as you can locate. Read all product descriptions assiduously and make your selection for download.

seven

Creating a
corporate
structure

You may be operating your business from a desk at a window in your living room overlooking the village green (as I do) but no one else on the Internet will know that. The impression you must always project in all you do is that of a professional corporate entity, and to accomplish this you will need to develop a corporate structure of your very own.

Make the most of your opportunities

For the purposes of this exercise we shall assume that you have decided to run with several opportunities in tandem to test out their potential. However, the guidelines provided on constructing a composite Web site are equally applicable should you decide to concentrate all your energies on a single idea.

If you're running with several, the mixture could be one of the following:

- three or more affiliate reseller programmes;
- your own idea plus several affiliate programmes;
- a selection of opportunities from those featured in Chapter 4.

Now you have to find ways of maximizing individual and overall potential in a pilot-testing operation that will take about three or four months. None of this is going to cost you a penny and, while you will need to work long and hard at the outset, your eventual input will consist of no more than an hour or so daily on promotion. The rest of the time you can devote to checking the returns and assisting your business to grow in other ways.

Here is what you have to do to maximize potential: pilot-test each of your potential opportunities individually; and design a composite Web site to house and promote the entire range.

Take individual sites for a test drive

If you are running with affiliate resellers, the majority of the programmes you have identified come complete with pre-designed Web sites and secure ordering facilities (ignore the handful that don't), and it is these Web sites that you will promote individually.

How you do this in a systematized manner is the subject matter of Chapter 8.

Constructing your composite Web site

To complement your campaign of individual programme promotion, you will create a composite, corporate Web site containing all of your wealth creators. This will double the thrust of your promotional activities and prove in time to be a vital cog in the overall marketing strategy.

Don't balk at the prospect of being asked to create a composite Web site. Don't worry if you've never designed anything before in your life. Do not be concerned if you can't even draw a straight line. Above all, don't worry about costs. Do a search and you'll find many sources where you can use Web page creation tools at no charge.

However, of all the available options you may encounter, I recommend Freeservers. As the name suggests, this service is free, and the easy-to-use 'wizard' design tools are superb – they can give you a product that is comparable with many professionally created Web sites that cost thousands to construct.

http://freeservers.com

Creating a strategy for construction

Let's turn our attention now to the creation of a strategy and flow chart for the layout of your proposed Web site:

▨ What will this entail?
▨ Which elements are we to include?
▨ How many pages will be required?

What you are in effect doing when you create a composite Web site is setting yourself up as a *mini* specialist opportunity house. It stands to reason therefore that you must include sufficient information and display it in such a way that visitors to your site can immediately identify who you are, what it is you do and how easy it is to do business with you.

Elements to include in the strategy are:

▨ *Name of the enterprise*, eg 'LensTop20', 'JimsWebStore', 'The Cyberspace Mall', 'Wealth_Wizard'. Whatever you decide, keep it short and to the point – no more than three words.
▨ *Brief mission statement* on what you are offering: specialist service, tangible merchandise, free Web sites, free training, etc.
▨ *Pic or illustration.* Could be a pic of yourself or an illustration relevant to the activity. Personal pics you will need to scan and import from your computer, but you can locate dozens of suitable illustrations from the toolbox of the 'wizard' you'll be using to create your pages. Simply download and insert the one you choose.
▨ *Hyperlinks* to each and every one of your opportunities. Follow the simple directions supplied in your page creation system and you will enable visitors to activate entry to *any* programme of their choice at a click of the mouse.
▨ *Special offer panel* to highlight a particular opportunity or promotional offer.
▨ *E-mail link* to allow visitors to contact you direct.
▨ *Autoresponder link* to reply to enquiries with a predetermined response.
▨ *Guestbook* to record visitor names, e-mail addresses and fax numbers.

Do not feel intimidated by the apparent immensity of the task facing you. 'Wizard' Web page creation systems lead you through the process step by step and in effect do all the work for you. With the following tools at your disposal you will create up to three pages within an hour:

- *Masthead generator*. Creates your trading name logo in a flash.
- *Copywriter*. Keys in your mission statement.
- *Image creator*. Positions your pic or illustration.
- *Hyperlink activator*. Just type in your programme URLs for immediate activation.
- *Gismos* to create your special offer panel and animated effects.
- *Links* to e-mail autoresponder are automatically activated.
- *Guestbook* created instantly with one click.
- *Metatag generator* to enhance your chances on positioning with the search engines.

How many pages and what is the split?

You could contain all of your information in a single page, but you will have a more effective Web site working for you if you spread it over three pages as follows:

- *home page*
  - masthead;
  - mission statement;
  - link to programmes page;
  - links to e-mail and autoresponder on final page;
  - special offer panel;
- *programmes page*
  - masthead (with linking copy);
  - list of hyperlinks to all affiliate programmes;
  - gismos such as weather forecast, astrology or lotto numbers, all of which you can get for free;
- *end page*
  - masthead;
  - 'thank you' message;
  - e-mail;
  - autoresponder.

Why are we designing the pages in this way?

Doing it this way provides visitors with choices; the information provided is in logical sequence; individual pagination is not convoluted; users can determine at a glance:

- who you are;
- what you do;
- how to contact you;
- how to sign up for your opportunities or order merchandise.

Add to all of this the fact that visitors are not to know that your operation is home-based.

Summarizing the benefits

So what are the specific benefits to be achieved by electing to create and operate your own Web pages, your very own composite Web site?

- You can market your business and sell its services online.
- You can do business 24 hours a day, every day.
- You can receive enquiries from all around the world.
- You can foster better customer relationships.
- You can answer prospects' questions and provide information instantly.
- You can compete on the same worldwide platform as international concerns.
- Prospects can browse your opportunities menu at leisure.
- Prospects can download and print out individual programme data.
- Prospects can sign up online.

View an actual Web site constructed using these techniques by visiting:

http://ewritelife.com

What to do next

The creation of your own corporate Web site is the key to broadcasting news of your enterprise worldwide and having new customers from far afield come directly to you. Before that can happen though, you must accomplish the following:

- If you don't have your own host computer, you can rent space for free from your ISP, which will normally provide you with 5 Mb of Web space as part of the basic deal (enough for almost 150 pages).

▓ Register the name of your Web site.
▓ Go online by placing your files on to the host computer.
▓ Promote your Web site's presence on the Internet.

How to go about promotion

As with any form of conventional advertising and marketing, competition to attract the attention of Internet users is positively fierce. Make early and consistent endeavours to promote your Web site's presence and ensure that every opportunity seeker cruising the Web has a fighting chance of finding your painstakingly created Web pages.

Connect to or sign up for every search engine and database available. You can accomplish this effortlessly by applying to Submit It and Promote It, which will then notify all of the major search engines that you have a new Web site (small fee involved here), or you can do it for free by submitting to the following sites:

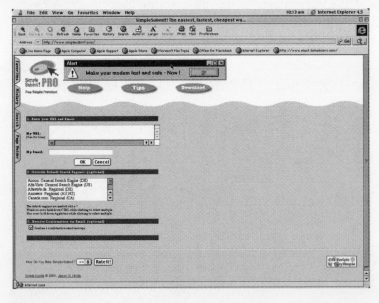

Figure 7.1 Submit your URLs free of charge to every major search engine (**http://www.simplesubmit.com**)

http://www.u-submit.com
http://www.simplesubmit.com

Immediately set about your campaign of exposure by ensuring that your Web site and e-mail addresses feature on your letterhead, business cards, compliments slips, invoices, statements, press advertising, print matter, etc. Thereafter apply yourself to keeping the information contained in your Web pages up to date.

Replicating the strategy

Having done it once, you have the option of stretching the reach of your global marketing by replicating your composite site through free tools provided by the following sources.

http://www.angelfire.com
http://www.tripod.com
http://www.theglobe.com

With another two or three replicated sites carrying the corporate message, your Internet presence will be considerably heightened.

Steps and stairs to a corporate identity

- Make sure you portray a professional image on the Internet. You are right up there among the major players.
- Promoting your opportunities individually and collectively pays off in the long run.
- Allow your pilot testing to run for up to four months. Use a focused Web site that will attract online purchases.
- Use 'wizard' Web page creation tools. They are of great benefit as they do the job for you.
- Submit your exclusive corporate Web site address(es) to every search engine on the Internet.

Exercise

Read over once again the example given in this chapter of the strategy devised for the creation of a composite Web site. Now apply yourself to devising a strategy for your own corporate Web site and complete the exercise by drawing up an appropriate flow chart. Allow for up to three Web pages to include:

- trading name;
- mission statement;
- profile of affiliate programmes;
- pic or illustration;
- active hyperlinks to bizops;
- links to e-mail and autoresponder.

Now add an inventive additional element of your own choosing.

eight

Devising the
Internet marketing strategy

It's all beginning to fit together now and the time is fast approaching for implementation of your Internet marketing strategy. To accomplish this, there are several ways in which you can promote your enterprise in cyberspace: some excellent, some good, some that can backfire on you if not properly used. How will your strategy shape up? We will now review all of the options in detail and arrive at a plan of action for consistent and effective promotion.

Open for business 24 hours a day

There is no early closing on the Internet. It's open for business seven days a week, every week. There are no time constraints either, because every second of every hour someone somewhere is buying online. You really can sell anything (well, *almost* anything) to anyone, anywhere, anytime.

Directing traffic to your Web sites

However you evolve, develop and implement your Internet marketing strategy, it will be done with one sole purpose in mind: *driving traffic to your Web sites*. You won't sell off the page in this business, regardless of whether the 'page' is an enticingly composed e-mail or a drum-beating classified ad. It simply does not happen that way on the Internet.

Unless your marketing persuades opportunity seekers to visit your Web sites (storefronts) and sample your merchandise (programmes), and tempts them to 'buy' on the spot (sign up electronically), your efforts will have been in vain and your business will rapidly fold through lack of interest.

Imagine instead that you were operating a string of high-street stores. You wouldn't under these circumstances expect your prospects to buy from you over the telephone without first visiting one of your stores, would you? Driving traffic to your Web site is essential in this business.

Consider all of your promotional options

Basically there are five options at your disposal and you should certainly use the first four in your marketing, but they must all be used correctly if you are to avoid the backfiring aspect touched on earlier. The final option is just that, an option, but an effective option nonetheless. The five options are:

- search engines;
- classified ad Web sites;
- effective e-mailing techniques;
- alternative media;
- promotional CD ROM.

How to position your sites with the search engines

Submission of your Web site addresses (individual and composite) isn't something you do just once, but every week without fail. Don't expect too much though in the way of prime positioning. You might just get some of your sites into the top

500 of a remote category, but you'll be lucky to make the top 5,000 of where you'd like to be – the opportunities category – unless you include keywords and metatags in all of your submissions.

For wealth creation programmes, for example, the keywords to use are 'wealth', 'fortune', 'millionaire', 'business', 'opportunity', 'success', 'money' and 'freedom'. The same keywords are used for metatags, but you never see them on the Web page. They are hidden persuaders that the Web page creation tools (and most submission services) will submit for you on request. Always take advantage of the offer *wherever* you come across it.

Classified ad sites can work wonders

These sites make a useful adjunct to your overall marketing mix and you can have as many of them as you wish for free. Your own offers will be featured in display ad format, *but* you can also use these classified ad sites to drive traffic to your main Web sites by inviting other Internet marketers to post their ads. You can accomplish this quite easily by regular e-mail shots directing users to a classified ad banner on your main site(s). So before they can post their ads, you have repeated opportunities to interest them in your primary propositions.

Advertise and send prospects directly to your ad sites

Alternatively, you can advertise and send people *directly* to your classified ad sites. When users post their ads, these sites acknowledge placement by an autoresponder 'welcome' message that will include complete details of your own opportunities.

An added bonus

You'll be able to give away free sites like your own to other users and in the process get two more opportunities to reach potential customers: 1) to obtain these free sites enquirers are directed to the classified ad banner on your main site(s) where they can view your opportunities while they are there; 2) when they sign up for a free site they also get the 'welcome' message.

Your own ad is the first they see

Your own display ad stays at the top of 16 disparate classified categories, so the very first ad prospects see is always *yours*!

How banners can drive traffic your way

You have the capability of posting banners on your classified sites to advertise any business you wish – and of participating in free banner programmes. This latter option will cost you a little money but it's worth it. You receive a commission any time anyone signs up under you.

The bottom line

Sign up for several of these classified sites because they will be of benefit to all of your online ventures and help you build up a stack of useful contacts. They cost nothing and are useful servants who will work non-stop for you.

E-mail – your number one selling tool

You'll be working with a small marketing budget, so how then do you obtain the best for less? By utilizing to its full advantage the most efficient promotional tool on the Internet: e-mail. E-mail marketing breaks down neatly into just two categories: 1) targeted; 2) untargeted.

Untargeted e-mailing is a waste of time

Untargeted marketing on the Internet normally takes the form of unsolicited bulk e-mail. Whether you do it yourself or hire one of the thousands of online blasting operators, it makes no difference, because it's simply a waste of time and effort.

Figure 8.1 TheMail.com pays you to receive, read and send e-mails (**http://themail.com**)

What is unsolicited e-mail?

If you don't have permission to send it, then it is unsolicited. Most ISPs do not allow this activity and they will close your account without notice as soon as the inevitable complaints start to trickle in. Don't risk it.

'Spamming' is bad netiquette

You are guilty of 'spamming' when you send unsolicited e-mail to addresses that have not agreed to receive commercial messages. Never indulge in spamming or you'll not only risk the reputation of your business; you'll get yourself into more trouble than you can imagine.

Targeted e-mail marketing is the only way

Targeted e-mail works best because you are talking to like-minded Internet users and you're doing it in an acceptable manner. Not only do you get much better results but you'll

107

never have to worry about being closed down or damaging your reputation as a home-based operator.

E-mailing to safe lists for free

'Safe lists' or 'opt-in lists' are general terms used to describe a group of Internet users who have agreed to receive promotional e-mail. Such lists can be obtained free of charge, rented or purchased and they all have their own rules for solicitation that should be studied and adhered to at all times.

However, exercise caution with safe list purchasing because there are some irresponsible Internet operators who simply 'harvest' or extract names and e-mail addresses from a variety of sources and then sell them on as safe lists. In the majority of cases these are not safe at all and using them puts you at risk of being labelled a spammer.

Why pay when you can get genuine safe lists for free?

There are free lists already set up on Yahoogroups, Globelists and Listbot that are specifically designed for Internet marketing. You simply subscribe to these lists and then start sending out e-mails advertising your product or service, using a key phrase in the subject line to gain attention.

With Globelists, subscribers have mail preference options: single mail or digest mode. Single means you will receive individual e-mails from the list; digest mode allows you to view all incoming messages in the form of a composite. It is a good practice in your early experience with Globelists to set your preference to digest mode. There are normally 25–50 ads per digest and you should read them all to give you a flavour of how other subscribers are promoting their opportunities.

Attempting to harvest e-mail addresses is illegal

Do not attempt to harvest the e-mail addresses of other advertisers and under no circumstances send any of them a direct promotional e-mail. Anyone caught spamming recognized safe lists will have their subscription cancelled immediately.

Do it right and you can advertise as often as you like

You may advertise as often as you wish on many of these lists and any restrictions to the contrary are stipulated at the time of subscription. Using an autoresponder to transmit your messages is considered bad form and so it is better that you compose your ad to include your Web site URL and/or contact details. Personally, I prefer people to contact me first before sending them to my Web sites.

So let's go!

Here is what to do:

1. Subscribe to each list via the URLs below.
2. Send out your initial promotional e-mail, placing the first destination on each list in the 'To' field and the remainder in 'Bcc'.
3. Read through a couple of the first digests you receive.
4. Create a file for your outgoing e-mails so that you can access, copy and send them all out again without retyping.
5. Bear in mind that the majority of the lists permit unlimited postings, enabling you to post your ads several times a day should you wish.
6. Look upon this as a long-term programme. Make it part of your daily routine.
7. Do not expect instant responses because the prime purpose is to keep your name in front of other users on a daily basis.
8. Keep on doing it and they will eventually respond.

Click on these to subscribe

First, you will have to register as a member.

http://www.yahoogroups.com
http://www.globelists.com
http://www.listbot.com

You will be allocated a user name and password for each of the groups and, while you are still at these sites, set about selecting those individual lists relevant to your particular marketplace.

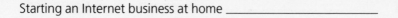

That's it; you are up and running, ready to blast out your promotional e-mails for free – and for evermore.

E-mailing to paid-for safe lists

This works basically the same as for free lists but you pay for the privilege. Paid-for lists are normally moderated to an extent and are more restrictive in terms of the number of times you can post daily.

Let the buyer beware…

Purchasers of paid-for lists should always carefully consider the source of origin – even to the extent of asking for references. Prices range from £5 upwards.

Recover your costs

If you do go in for buying safe lists (and this is something I would not necessarily recommend), you have an opportunity to recover your costs through introductions. Just two or three referrals should be enough to pay your own entry fee.

The following paid-for operators are OK and the only ones I would endorse with any degree of confidence:

http://www.flintelmarketing.com
http://themailblaster.com/safelist.html
http://www.theskynetwork.com

Using alternative media strategically

You're left now with two very useful marketing tools to include somewhere in your overall strategy: 1) generating traffic with free reports; and 2) signing off your e-mails with a sales message.

Generate traffic with free reports

These are special reports written by experts on every conceivable aspect of Internet training. They are not surprisingly very popular on the Internet and now there are programmes that will generate traffic for you by offering *free* reports. Once you subscribe you will have links back to your site(s) on thousands of pages and reports all over the Internet:

- *Leading Edge Reports*
  http://www.Websitings.com
- *Link Reward*
  http://www.linkreward.com

You can obtain and employ these for free. Use one opportunity or several disparate ones. Use the report nets to draw attention to your site through e-mail ads or classifieds. Put a link on your main Web site(s) for all your reports.

Sign off your e-mails with a sales message

On every e-mail you send out into the stratosphere, make sure you tag on a 'signature' that sells one or more of your opportunities. Here's an example of how to do this effectively:

Spam and they'll close you down! Play it safe with the 60k OPT-IN Mailing List. Blast out your e-mails once a week with just ONE click to 1000s of safe, eager opportunity seekers. Lifetime Membership only US$24.95. Sign up fast'n'easy online and you can mail out straightaway! **http://moneytree.olm.net/60kopt432.htm**

Get it all together on a CD ROM

You can commit a whole variety of computer files to CD ROM: text, graphics, video, animation, etc. However (as in the case of constructing your composite Web site), it is essential to draw up an appropriate strategy before commencing.

Trim the costs by preparing in advance

Perhaps at this early stage you don't feel sufficiently confident about creating your own promotional CD ROM. Should that be the case, hand the project over to someone who does. However, if you decide to use an external source, make every endeavour to handle as much of the pre-production work as you can manage in-house. You will save money if you do.

Get it all together

Efficient pre-production is all down to advance preparation: strategy, 'shooting script' and collation of all the required elements (graphics, pics, illustrations, video clips, animation, etc). You will also need to compose an appropriate commentary to accompany the visual aspects. There's nothing difficult about any of this; it's just a matter of application.

Developing the strategy

Let's demonstrate the pre-production process by turning our attention back to the plan we devised for constructing a Web site. We'll include the same elements (saving some time and effort) but also add a few new ones. The list will look something like this:

- company name, etc;
- brief mission statement;
- pic/illustration;
- video clip;
- hyperlink to main Web site;
- hyperlinks to *all* affiliate programmes;
- e-mail responding facility;
- link to autoresponder.

Let's see how all of this shapes up in the 'shooting script', which (despite the arty title) should be simple, brief and straightforward in its execution. You are not about to conceive the production script for a major motion picture, only for a promotional piece, the scenes and settings of which are to be set out succinctly, step by step.

Production script for your very own promotional CD ROM

1. *Opening frames* – letters and characters come together from different angles and directions to form your trading name in an animated fashion.
2. Cut to clear screen where your *mission statement* (25-word maximum) appears – word following word, line by line – in telex-type format.
3. Dissolve to light pastel-colour background featuring interactive bullet-pointed hyperlinks:
   - *main Web site* (accessed through integrated plug-in, say Shockwave);
   - *opportunity Web sites* (up to 20 in total);
   - *greetings from the CEO* (ie *you*, on video);
   - *special premium offer* (ie free reports to sign-ups online);
   - *e-mail* (also accessed through the Web site);
   - *autoresponder* (ditto).
4. When accessed, the hyperlinks give the recipient options to flip back and forth from one Web site to another. Once a particular opportunity is clicked and viewed, the presentation reverts to the pastel background housing all of the features. The opportunity just viewed is highlighted, enticing the recipient to move on to other opportunities. All of the affiliate Web sites contain essential secure ordering facilities.
5. Ends with *freeze-frame*: logo and thank-you message.

That's really all there is to it. Take the trouble, save some money and create a promotional CD ROM you'll be proud to send to your customers.

To summarize:

- Create your strategy.
- Develop a script for production purposes.
- Write an appropriate commentary.
- Collate all graphics, pics, video clips, etc.
- Call in professional help if you need it.

Who do you send your promotional CD ROM to?

That's easy: hot prospects who just need another nudge to sign up. You'll find that many of them sign up for several programmes on the spot on receipt of your CD. Why? Because very, very few of your competitors will be so imaginative.

Selling on the Internet

When you evolve your Internet marketing strategy, you also create your sales policy. Selling on the Internet is similar to traditional mail-order selling in that you never get to meet your customers. You avoid personal interaction and presentation, and consequently it is harder to strike up dialogue and get your message across.

Compensate for lack of personal contact

Successful Networkers turn this perceived downside on its head by utilizing every aspect of electronic interaction to the fullest advantage in every tool they use. Striking up an initial dialogue might prove slow to begin with, but if you persist the response factor will soon start to improve – and with good reason. You are not indulging in scatter-gun marketing here; you are talking to like-minded Internet users who share an affinity with your proposition.

Compensate for lack of personal presentation

How you talk electronically to your prospects is crucial, and so it is important that:

- your Web sites are professionally constructed and user-friendly;
- your information is clear, concise and honest;
- your copy platforms are compelling;
- your sales messages are persuasive;
- you use your autoresponders to keep the dialogue going.

Golden rules you must observe

Observe these golden rules at all times:

- *Never spam.* They'll shut you down if you do.
- *Never send out promotional e-mails that lack sincerity or conviction.* You'll just blow away your credibility.
- *Never promise what you cannot deliver.* If you do, you'll lose your integrity.
- *Never argue with a prospect.* You'll lose out if you do.
- *Never knock the competition.* Don't talk about them; learn from them quietly.
- *Never leave a lost sale thinking it's lost for ever.* The deal may not have been right for the prospect this time but the next one might be.
- *Never take rejection to heart.* You won't appreciate your successes until you have experienced the odd loss or two.
- *Never fail to keep your sales records up to date.* How else will you know how you're doing?

Steps and stairs to Internet marketing

- Once you have your chosen programmes in position and you've built your Web sites, create an integral Internet marketing strategy.
- Be under no illusion: driving traffic to your Web sites is the cornerstone of your plan.
- Use all the available options for promotion – but use them correctly for total effectiveness.
- When submitting to a search engine, always insert relevant keywords.
- Sign up for several free classified ad Web sites. They'll work for you all day, every day.
- Study and learn the techniques that make e-mail the most effective promotional tool on the Internet – and *never* spam or they'll close you down.
- Free reports and 'signatures' are good alternative media.
- Create your own promotional CD ROM and send it to hot prospects.
- Observe the golden rules for selling on the Internet.

Exercise

You've guessed it. Develop a strategy for the production of a promotional CD ROM. Do it on the basis that you will do all pre-production in-house and then hand the project over to an external source for finishing, polishing and copying.

nine

Managing
information

Information begins to build up rapidly once you really get going in this business, and because it's coming at you from every direction it can just as easily drift away from you unless measures are taken to organize it all efficiently. This brief chapter shows you how to manage your information with the minimum of effort and the maximum of efficiency.

Create a working master list

Your first job will be to make out a list of every aspect of your operational activities so that incoming information can be correctly apportioned. Here are the main areas, but you can add to these as your business develops:

- income-generating Web sites
  - individual programmes;
  - composites;
- classified ad Web sites
  - income-generating;
  - promotional;
- Web sites under construction (those still to be completed);
- e-mail addresses (sundry e-mail accounts);
- autoresponders (you should have several at your command);
- user names and passwords (to gain access to sites);
- virtual office suites (for day-to-day electronic processing);
- commission scales (for each affiliate programme);
- sub-sites (to access hits / commissions earned);

- electronic tools
  - Web site address submission;
  - ad submission;
  - bulk ad mailers;
  - bulk e-mailers;
  - ad copy storage;
- safe (opt-in) lists (for spam-free posting);
- progress charting
  - daily ad/e-mail postings;
  - weekly ad/e-mail postings.

Your best bet is to contain these listings in a binder (preferably one with plastic sleeves) to carry around with you when you're away from the computer.

Why categorizing your money-making activities is vital

Be sure to include in your listings all the money-making aspects of your opportunities; some will be commission-only on sales, some sales commission plus additional revenue on referrals and some both of these together with incentive bonuses. Don't go into detail. Just include enough information to remind you where your profit centres are. An example is given in the box below.

Designate your classified ad sites

Your collection of classified ad Web sites will be used mainly for promotional purposes but several will also be revenue producers. Designate them all accordingly to ensure that you don't miss out on accrued income (reseller programme contractors do not always tell you when you're making money out of them!).

Why would you have Web sites under construction?

Aside from the composite sites you build to house your sundry opportunities, you should also sign up for several spares. These

Revenue-generating Web sites

Virtualis (virtual systems)
http://www.virtualis.com/vr2/jgreen2 (sales)
http://www.virtualis.com/vr2/jgreen2/reps (affiliate sign-ups)

JDD Publishing (*Insider Internet Marketing* book)
http://www.bizWeb2000.com/d5315.htm

VenerNet (server systems)
http://www.vener.net/rep2/jimgreen-info.shtm
(account ex sign-up)
http://www.vener.net/rep2/jimgreen-server.shtm
(sales)

Smart Money Group (ghost downline builder / recruitment)
http://www.smartmoneygroup.com/SMG/ghostmem/ JGO152.htm

Ezze.Net (creating home-based ISPs)
http://www.ezze.net/affiliates/28699

MyFreeOfficeOnline (sundry / referrals)
http://myfreeoffice.com/jimsWebstore

Marketwize (software programmes / recruitment)
http://www.marketwize.com/biz/ware/m45r/index. html

RealCall (Internet software / recruitment)
http://www.realcall.net/internet

Multilinks (free Web sites)
http://multilinks.net/index.shtml?10966

The Duplicator (downline Internet information product)
http://www.theduplicator.com/vip.cgi/jim333

Wise Old Mule Club (downline Internet information product)
http://www.wisemuleclub.com/d/JG1118.html

Site Sell (5 Pillar Club – Internet know-how)
http://www.sitesell.com/success66.html

Magic Learning (learning systems sales / reseller programme)
http://www.magiclearning.com/cgi/members/JG51079

will provide you with options. For example, use them for new opportunities coming on stream or to promote special offers.

Gaining easy access to your e-mail accounts

You will be using a number of e-mail accounts concurrently, and you want to be able to get at them quickly. List individual facilities for easy access.

List your autoresponders

These valuable communication tools will come into their own when you start to promote your programmes on a regular basis. Make sure you know where to locate them.

Why you need to list user names and passwords

User names and passwords aren't necessarily the same for all programmes and promotional accounts (the rules vary). Avoid wasting time searching for names and passwords among mounds of paperwork. List them.

Switching swiftly from one virtual suite to another

Your virtual office suites offer varying facilities and you will use all of them. List these so that you can rapidly identify which suite offers what facilities as you seamlessly switch from one application to another. An example of such a listing is:

- Web site;
- Web site promotion tools;
- e-mail facility;
- autoresponder;
- search engine;
- word processor;
- database;
- spreadsheets;
- secure ordering facilities;
- shopping cart.

Keeping an eye on your commission scales

Commission scales can cause confusion unless you list them all for reference.

Sub-sites tell you how you're doing

Certain opportunities will have sub-sites where you may view your revenue statistics on demand. List those sub-sites.

Your safe lists at a glance

Group all of your safe opt-in e-mail lists (see the example in the box below) for ease of daily and weekly promotional postings.

Itemize all of the promotional tools you use

When you've done all the spadework and your business is up and running, you will be spending so much of your time on promotion that it's easy to get into a rut using manual applications. The tendency is to forget that secreted in your computer are a host of tools you put there to do it all for you automatically. Include all of these tools in your listings – just to remind you from time to time of their existence and applicability.

Charting progress for your marketing strategy

Never trust your memory to prompt you on daily and weekly promotional functions. Write it all down. Then you'll be able to chart progress on your overall marketing activities. An example is given in the box below.

E-mail daily postings

varantmkg@egroups.com
(via **jim@megan62.freeserve.co.uk**)
mlmworks@egroups.com
(via **jim@megan62.freeserve.co.uk**)
a_netcash@egroups.com
(via **jim@megan62.freeserve.co.uk**)
supersafe@listbot.com
(via **jim@megan62.freeserve.co.uk**)
the_professional@egroups.com
(via **jim@megan62.freeserve.co.uk**)
NoLimitAds@onelist.com
(via **jim@megan62.freeserve.co.uk**)
free-home-based-ads@egroups.com
(via **jim@megan62.freeserve.co.uk**)
BizOpClassifieds@listbot.com
(via **jimsWebstore@The-mail.com**)
theList2000@globelists.com
(via **jimsWebstore@The-mail.com**)
(via **stacy340@hotmail.com**)
freeads@globelists.com
(via **jimsWebstore@The-mail.com**)
(via **stacy340@hotmail.com**)

E-mail weekly postings

60kOpt_In@listbot.com
(via **jim@megan62.freeserve.co.uk**)
ListID@listbot.com
(via **jim@megan62.freeserve.co.uk**)
(via **stacy340@hotmail.com**)

Weekly ads posting

Flintel
Blaster
Classified connection
Wise Wolf + Mikes List + MC tools

Take time out to organize the paperwork

Even though your enterprise is computer-based, paperwork just seems to keep on mounting up and there's little you can do about it. You could of course house all of the information in your computer, but (unless you use a laptop) that won't help when you're out and about and need to refer to something urgently.

What sorts of paperwork are we talking about here?

Not a lot fortunately, and confined to these essential categories: 1) programme data; 2) new business opportunities. Keep your paperwork to a minimum so that it is always transportable.

Be consistent in performing regular chores

It takes time to record accurately all of the details previously discussed, but it will be a pointless exercise unless you perform all of the following regular chores with consistency. They are chores that you must accomplish daily or weekly, so that you are ready to take advantage of every opportunity to build your business:

- e-mail checking (daily);
- ads and promotional e-mail postings (daily and weekly);
- affiliate contact (as required);
- Web site(s) updating (as required);
- revenue checks (weekly – and not at all boring).

Steps and stairs to managing information

■ Managing accumulated information is crucial to the success of your home-based Internet business.

■ Be comprehensive in the compilation of your working master lists but don't make them too complex.

■ Remember that several of your programmes have more than one profit centre.

■ Classified ad Web sites can generate income as well as promoting your opportunities.

■ List all of these: e-mail accounts, autoresponders, user names and passwords, virtual office suites and promotion tools.

■ Organize your paperwork efficiently.

■ Make provision for charting the progress of your marketing activities.

Exercise

Using as a benchmark the guidelines given in this chapter, devise your own system for managing incoming information.

ten

Maintaining
progress

Let's examine the basic skills and personal qualities you will need to develop (and indeed *enhance* as you progress) in your quest to be Networking successfully here, there and everywhere.

Strategic overview for the home-based operator

Here is your basic mission statement in three straight, short, crisp lines:

■ Networking is a way of working, not just a job.
■ Networking produces opportunities for manageable, sustainable growth.
■ Networking is a good option for avoiding 9–5 drudgery.

That's all you need to think about. Now start planning...

Basic qualities you'll need to develop

You'll need:

■ self-motivation;
■ the ability to work without close supervision;
■ quantifiable time-management skills;
■ flexibility;
■ resilience;

- self-reliance;
- excellent communication and interpersonal skills;
- experience of electronic interaction;
- the ability to cope with conflicting demands under one roof (work and home);
- keyboard skills;
- knowledge of modem applications;
- competence in electronic mail facilities;
- the ability to conduct online discussions;
- effective use of Web sites;
- ad copywriting skills;
- report writing skills;
- telephone communication skills;
- self-management skills (eg interactive CD ROM learning capability, time management).

Getting off to the best possible start

You've had your test run on all your chosen opportunities, monitored progress, assessed and reviewed results to date. What happens next? How do you go about ensuring that you get off to the best possible start? By developing a clear appreciation of certain essential personal qualities that make for successful Networking in the Information Age.

Empowerment through self-motivation

Empowerment to engage in Networking comes from self-motivation. There is no other way. You must be absolutely certain of your goals, in the short and in the long term. Why else would you want to work on your own? What else could possibly inspire you?

In the longer term, think about whether you will *consistently* enjoy your new working arrangement, whether the business will still offer variety, stimulation and opportunity for personal development and whether you will be able to combat the possible risk of isolation and loneliness.

Being in when you're out

It stands to reason that you're not going to be stuck at your desk all of the time. You'll have to be out and about some of the time. How can you control the business and avoid missing important contacts when you're not there? In other words, how can you be in when you're out?

Thankfully, because you're a Networker, you have information technology and the Internet as reliable, indispensable co-workers to look after your affairs when you're not around:

- mobiles to keep in touch;
- answering machines to take your calls;
- e-mail and fax to receive urgent messages;
- the Internet to accept the sales that bring in the cash.

Protecting your most important asset

Your ability to earn income is your most important asset, and there are two ways to protect it if you decide to make Networking from home a full-time career: 1) by way of an income protection plan; 2) by way of a critical illness policy.

No one working alone likes to think too much or too often about these matters, but make some provision. An income protection plan provides replacement income, and a critical illness policy pays out a lump sum on diagnosis of serious illness.

Remove the hobby aspect from your networking

Your author is a Networker (and as prone to temptation as anyone else) with an all-consuming passion for vintage films. The *Corel All-Movie Guide* CD ROM is always locked away securely in a desk drawer during working hours. Otherwise...

Reducing stress through effective time management

And here's how to do it:

- Don't make appointments without first consulting your diary.
- Don't work long hours unless you are being rewarded accordingly.
- Don't be afraid to reject opportunities that are unprofitable.
- Don't be so inflexible in your scheduling that you can't handle last-minute demands on your time.
- Don't try to keep everything in your head; write it all down.
- Don't delude yourself that you're Networking when catching up on the latest cricket or football scores.
- Don't let a day end without making out an action list for tomorrow.

Harness the power

Here are two Networker Web sites for you to visit. The first – **http://www.gilgordon.com/hub.htm** – permits access to a variety of useful resource papers, some free and some that you have to pay a little to download. It includes:

- AT&T *Telework Guide*;
- Bell Atlantic *Teleworking Guide*;
- Siemens's *Managing Your Business Effectiveness with Teleworking*.

The other Web site is that of the Entrepreneur's Home Office Magazine.

www.homeofficemag.com/

It publishes a regular stream of useful reports:

- Master of your own domain.
- Tip of the day.
- Solutions.
- Internet freebies.

- Be your own boss!
- Cash in with money hunters.
- Homezone.
- Power tools.
- Money.
- Marketing.
- Get organized.
- Resources.

eleven

Duplicating and **replicating your master plan**

This is where you begin to duplicate and replicate your master plan for creating a successful home-based Internet business. Remember your corporate Web site? Now you are about to take it a vital stage further, and you have a choice to make.

New master Web site

You will either enhance the existing content (if you are staying with affiliate programmes) *or* create entirely new content (if you choose to specialize). Stick with Freeservers (they're the most professional), but be more adventurous on this occasion and employ several more of the sophisticated tools on offer. Don't overdo the cosmetics though, just sufficient to give your prime site a touch of class. Spend as much time as you have to on this exercise and, if you don't get it right first time, try again.

Bear in mind that you are doing this to promote your products or service and to get other people to replicate your proposition, pay you and promote for you.

Promotional e-mailing

Direct all your e-mailing activities from this point on to daily promotion.

Classified ads

Now all the hard work you put into setting up and developing your range of classified ad Web sites is about to pay off. Once again, focus your ad activities on your proposition.

Duplicating and replicating the formula

If you concentrate exclusively on promoting affiliate reseller programmes, you will be in a position to forge straight ahead on duplication and replication. However, in a business of your own choosing or creation, that may not be possible. The majority of the 35 opportunities featured in Chapter 4 are very much hands-on and require you to become highly proficient in their marketing before you can think of duplicating and replicating the formula. With a number of others though, you could start the process almost immediately.

Replication and duplication can be effected in three ways. Let's briefly examine each in turn.

Building up the downlines

The more successful you are in getting people to sign up for your wealth-creating opportunities, the more recruits you will have joining your army of co-workers. They will duplicate what you do, make some money and, as a logical sequence of events, make you even more money.

Referrals programme

Your ever-growing downlines will then become the base for starting up your own referral programme. What's a referral programme? It is the simple process of informing on a regular basis those who have already signed up for one or more of your opportunities (your downlines) about additional propositions you have coming on stream. If they're happy with what you've already introduced them to, the chances are high that they'll sign up for these new opportunities too.

Persuading others to do what you do

With the first two elements under way, you are now in the fast lane in the duplication and replication of your success system. Here's where you begin to persuade your army of co-workers to build their own downlines and referral programmes. This is how the Internet marketing gurus become extremely rich.

How to make your site irresistible to the search engines

You can make your master Web site(s) totally irresistible to the major search engines by adopting the outrageously successful technique employed by an anonymous Netpreneur who turns over an incredible *32 million dollars a day*. What's his secret? Well, he's got two actually...

Web aliases

Let us say that you've invested some money in the purchase of an exclusive domain name such as **http://fredsmart.com**. You add the metatags and keywords, and you promote your exclusive URL consistently and religiously on every available search engine week in, week out. But nothing happens. The only hits recorded on your swish counter are your own. What do you do? Here's what the 32-million-dollar-a-day man does. He invents Web aliases that concentrate on the core purpose of the business and, in so doing, he persuades the search engines to position his Web sites exactly where he wants them to be. Your author has a domain name that he didn't purchase but that pulls reasonably well. However, since switching to Web aliases the hits are increasing and multiplying by the day.

The site **http://dmapower/wealth_wizard.com** developed not just one but six Web aliases:

- **http://riches.radpages.com**;
- **http://radpages.com/riches**;
- **http://riches.Webdare.com**;
- **http://Webdare.com/riches**;
- **http://riches.tophonors.com**;
- **http://tophonors.com/riches**.

You can obtain your Web aliases completely free of charge at the following site, compliments of the 32-million-dollar-a-day man:

http://Webalias.com

Mirror pages

Your final act in mastering duplication and replication is to create 'mirror pages' for your master Web site(s). It's like splitting £10 notes, and really foxes the search engines. There are several good books around on creating mirror pages. Buy one and master this simple and highly profitable act of replication.

Give freely unto others...

Soon you will be on your way, and soon you will be put to the test on the single most important ingredient in the formula for creating lasting success in a home-based Internet business of your own making. What's that? Your willingness to share your good fortune and, in turn, hand over your secrets to others so that they may do what you have just done. So important is this that you should always bear in mind that what's yours today belongs to someone else tomorrow.

This book may have cost you a few pounds but its contents are worth much more, so share the philosophy with anyone you think could use some help. Let me leave you with an eternal truth: you only take out and *retain* what you first put in. Think about it.

Steps and stairs to get you there

Making money on the Internet is all down to locating and recognizing opportunities and adhering to the formula you've learnt in this book. You have been introduced to opportunities you wouldn't find anywhere else. Now it's up to you:

- Will you grasp the nettle?
- Will you take immediate action?
- Will you be one of the new breed of home-based Internet business owners?
- Will you still be thinking it over 12 months from now?

glossary

ad submission tool   Electronic device that e-mails ads to unlimited locations.

application service provider   Internet user who hosts Web-based applications on his or her Web site.

autoresponder   Device to receive and respond to e-mailed messages automatically.

bizop   Universally accepted Internet jargon for 'business opportunities'.

bulk mailer   E-mails out to masses of locations in a single application.

clip art   Electronic graphics that can be imported or down-loaded to any computer.

Common Gateway Interface (CGI)   Popular programming language used to build interactive Web sites.

desktop publishing   The design and production of literature using the resources of a domestic computer.

discussion board   A Web site where messages may be read or posted.

domain name   The electronic name tag for a Web site.

downline   Term applied to groups of people who have agreed to participate actively in a given Internet venture.

e-book   Electronically generated book.

e-zine   Electronically generated online magazine.

freeware   Internet tools that are obtainable free of charge.

information-on-demand Provision of information that can be instantly downloaded.

keywords Key words and phrases used to enhance a Web site's chances of higher positioning in search engine listings.

metatag Hidden persuaders (keywords) injected into but never visible on Web sites.

metatag generator The electronic device that implants metatags.

moderated list Safe or opt-in list that is regularly monitored. Usually allows only limited postings on a daily or weekly basis.

netiquette The rules of etiquette adhered to by responsible Networkers.

Netpreneur Internet entrepreneur.

Networker Anyone who works the Internet for profit.

niche solution provider Someone who supplies 'complete solutions' for a designated market by offering software tools, lead generation tools, articles, etc.

opt-in list List of Networkers who have agreed to receive e-mails on business opportunities.

password Code to allow access to Web sites etc.

reseller programme Any Internet programme that pays affiliates to represent its services.

safe list Alternative term for opt-in list.

shareware Similar to freeware but requiring a subsidy from users.

signature Promotional message tagged to the foot of e-mails.

snail mail Standard conventional mail.

spamming Sending out unsolicited e-mail to unsuspecting recipients.

teleworking What Networkers do.

user name Prescribed identity for Internet users.

virtual office suite Electronic suite providing the Internet user with a variety of essential promotional tools.

Web alias Web site address alias to enhance search engine positioning.

Useful **Web sites**

Free URL submission at these sites

http://www.u-submit.com
http://www.simplesubmit.com

Affiliate reseller programmes

http://www.wealthbuildingsolutions.com/?JIM101299
http://www.cashflowclubonline.com/?JIM101299
http://www.cashflowloanonline.com/?JIM101299
http://activemarketplace.com
http://www.sixfigureincome.com
http://www.virtualis.com
http://www.ezze.net
http://www.sitesell.com
http://www.bizweb2000.com
http://www.post-master.net
http://www.magiclearning.com
http://www.one-and-only.com
http://cognigen.net/getnext.cgi
http://www.clickbank.com
http://www.amazon.co.uk

Ideas for a home-based Internet business operation

http://www.rjcampbell.com/
http://ehost.domainzero.com
http://unclaimeddomains.com
http://www.infowave2000.com
http://www.AssociatePrograms.com
http://www.SuccessArsenal.com
http://www.Internetmarketingchallenge.com
http://www.universalthread.com
http://ultimateadvertisingclub.com
http://www.tunza-products.com/classified/ads.html
http://www.linkomatic.com
http://www.sellyourbrainfood.com

http://www.angieslist.com
http://www.cgi-resources.com
http://www.cgi101.com
http://www.thewarriorgroup.com
http://www.press-releases.net
http://www.searchengineforums.com/bin/Ultimate.cgi
http://www.goto.com/d/about/advertisers/faq.jhtml
http://www.becanada.com/
http://www.pair.com
http://www.write101.com
http://www.aspnews.com/
http://www.lifestylespub.com/clickbank/?hop=jjjones/lifestyles
http://www.anaconda.net/
http://www.AffiliateTracking.com/
http://www.animfactory.com/affiliate.html
http://www.oska.com/tahni.pht
http://www.leads4insurance.com/

Twenty-two e-mail facilities you can have for free

http://conk.com
http://hotmail.com
http://www.themail.com
http://lycos.com
http://mailcity.com
http://excite.com
http://netaddress.usa.net
http://www.yahoo.co.uk
http://eudoramail.com
http://postmaster.co.uk
http://onlymail.com
http://thedorm.com
http://hempseed.com
http://juno.com
http://www.uk2.net
http://netscape.net
http://theglobe.com
http://www.bizland.com
http://nightmail.com
http://www.bigfoot.com
http://www.affiliatesupport.com/ascmail.htm
http://www.teamon.com

Free electronic tools

http://www.BizWeb2000.com
http://www.thewarriorgroup.com/utrack.zip

index